Angus&Robertson

An imprint of HarperCollins*Publishers*, Australia

First published in Australia by Angus & Robertson Publishers in 1940
Reprinted 14 times
Reset and rearranged in 1960
Reprinted 11 times
New edition published in 1982
Reprinted 5 times
Commemorative edition published in 1986
Classic edition published in 1990
Reprinted in 1991, 1992, 1994, 1995, 1996, 1997, 1999 (twice)
by HarperCollins*Publishers* Pty Limited
ACN 009 913 517
A member of the HarperCollins*Publishers* (Australia) Pty Limited Group
http://www.harpercollins.com.au

HarperCollins*Publishers*

25 Ryde Road, Pymble, Sydney, NSW 2073, Australia
31 View Road, Glenfield, Auckland 10, New Zealand
77-85 Fulham Palace Road, London W6 8JB, United Kingdom
Hazelton Lanes, 55 Avenue Road, Suite 2900, Toronto, Ontario M5R 3L2
and 1995 Markham Road, Scarborough, Ontario M1B 5M8, Canada
10 East 53rd Street, New York NY 10022, USA

National Library of Australia Cataloguing-in-Publication data:

Gibbs, May, 1877–1969.
The complete adventures of Snugglepot and Cuddlepie.
ISBN 0 207 16738 9.
I. Title. (Series : Australian children's classics (Angus&Robertson).)
A823.2.

Printed in Singapore by Tien Wah Press on 100 gsm Woodfree

46 45 44 43   99 00 01 02

Amber Donaldson

CONTENTS

The Gum Blossom Ballet

The Complete Adventures of

Snugglepot and Cuddlepie

Written and illustrated by
MAY GIBBS

Angus&Robertson
An imprint of HarperCollins*Publishers*

Snugglepot and Cuddlepie

HERE are the adventures of Snugglepot and Cuddlepie. They were foster-brothers, and this is how it came about.

When Cuddlepie was very small—that is, when he had only been out of the bud a few hours—a great wind arose and, lifting him out of his mother's arms, carried him far across the tops of many trees and left him in a spider-web.

This saved his life, but again he nearly lost it, for a short-sighted old bird, mistaking him for a grub, was about to eat him up, when a Nut, beholding, shouted "Bird! Bird! mind the snake."

The old bird, very frightened, flew away. Then the kind Nut climbed up the spider-web, lifted up the little cold, weeping baby and gently carried him home.

Now this was the home of Snugglepot, and the kind Nut was his father.

Here then lived Cuddlepie side by side with Snugglepot, and they grew strong and fat as you see them in the pictures.

One day a wise old Kookaburra came to the neighbourhood. All the Blossoms and Nuts crowded in to hear him speak.

He said, "I am old! I have travelled! I have seen Humans! Humans are strong as the Wind, swift as the River, fierce as the Sun. They can scratch one stick upon another and, lo, there will be a Bush Fire. They love the Fire. The male Human carries it about in his skin and the smoke comes out of his nostrils. They whistle like the birds; they are cruel as the snake. They have many skins which they take off many times. When all the skins are off the Human looks like a pale frog."

1

Those Strange Humans

Now Snugglepot and Cuddlepie were scared all over to hear of these things, so they went often to listen to the wise Kookaburra.

"These Humans," said **Mr Kookaburra**, "are as bad as bad, but there must be bad things in this world as well as good. It would be very awkward for me if there were no snakes to eat."

And Snugglepot and Cuddlepie thought very much about it all.

One day they asked Mr Blue-cap Wren if it were all true. "Quite," said he, "I have some relations living in the Sydney Domain, and I know."

"I want to see a Human," said Snugglepot.

"In the distance," said Cuddlepie.

The Lecture

The Journey Begins

One very hot night, when the Cicadas were singing so loudly that Snugglepot couldn't hear his father snoring, he and Cuddlepie crept out of bed and out of the house.

"Where are you going?" asked Cuddlepie.

"To see the Humans," said Snugglepot.

"Only in the distance," pleaded Cuddlepie. Then they began their journey. When they had walked a long way Snugglepot said, "It is nearly day, let us pretend to be birds so that no one will know us."

"Yes," said Cuddlepie; "but we can't fly."

They found an old nest and took the feathers from it and dressed themselves in them. When the Sun rose they were far from home. In the little home the kind father and mother and

The Home of Snugglepot and Cuddlepie

A Busy Highroad

An Awkward Mistake

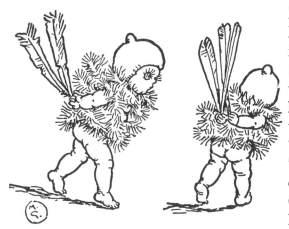

little baby brother had looked out all night long into the darkness, but Snugglepot and Cuddlepie were far away. No one had known them, but all who passed them had said, "What strange birds!" Then Snugglepot had chuckled in his neck, and Cuddlepie had chuckled in his neck too. All day they walked upon a busy highroad. See them in the picture—Snugglepot is leaning out of a nut helping himself to a bun. It is a grass-root bun.

At last it grew dark and, being very tired, they went to sleep in a hollow tree. Now it so happened that a very greedy Owl lived in this tree. When Cuddlepie went to sleep Snugglepot had covered him with all the feathers to keep him cosy. So when the greedy Owl opened his eyes the first thing he blinked at was Snugglepot's little fair body lying in the moonlight.

"Pink mouse! Pink mouse!

and I'm so hungry," muttered the greedy Owl. Then he pounced upon Snugglepot and flew with him out into the sky.

At the flutter of wings Cuddlepie awoke. When he saw the terrible thing that was happening he screamed aloud, "Take me! Take me! I don't want to be left. I would rather be eaten with Snugglepot than live alone without him." But the greedy Owl flew on, away, away till he was but a speck in the distance.

Poor little Cuddlepie tried to run after them, but the tears in his eyes were so big that he could not see which way to go.

Now the greedy Owl had a greedy wife, and in his haste to get his pink mouse out of her way he had not noticed that he was carrying a Gumnut Baby, and not a pink mouse at all. When

he saw his mistake he was so shocked that he let Snugglepot fall. Down, down, down he tumbled, right through the window into an Ant's house. A tired night-nurse saw him coming, but before she could do anything he had crashed in and killed several babies. This was a blessing for Snugglepot, but it was sadly hard on the baby ants.

"I'm so sorry," said Snugglepot.

"It can't be helped," said the Nurse.

Snugglepot falls into an Ant's house

"What will their mother say?" asked Snugglepot, brushing tears from his eyes.

"She won't know," said the Nurse, "we have three hundred babies in the house."

The Nurse was a kind person. When Snugglepot had told his story she patted his back and said, "I have a sister who works for a Blossom Lady near here. They will help you." She pointed the way to Snugglepot and he soon found the house.

It was now early morning and the Blossom was taking her bath, but when the Nurse's sister gave her Snugglepot's message she hastily dressed and came to see him. While they were talking a bird flew in with the news that a poor little Gumnut Baby was down in the road, weeping and crying out in great distress.

"It's my brother," cried Snugglepot.

"Then come," said the bird, "get on my back", and she flew with him straight to where poor little Cuddlepie was wandering. When he saw Snugglepot, Cuddlepie ran into his arms and held him so tightly about the neck that Snugglepot was nearly choked. Snugglepot did not like kissing in public, so he said, "We must thank kind Mrs Bird."

"Fantail is my name," said she.

"Mrs Fantail," said Snugglepot, "can we do anything to please you, ma'am?"

Mrs Fantail was rather a gadabout, so she said, "Yes, I'd be so obliged if you'd step up and mind my eggs for me while I pay some calls."

Snugglepot and Cuddlepie were glad to be of use. They climbed up into her nest and she went off gaily. She was a long time away.

"I think," said Snugglepot, "these eggs are getting cold."

Mr Lizard Helps

"We'd better sit on them," said Cuddlepie.

"Sit light, then," said Snugglepot. "I will," said Cuddlepie; so they both sat on the eggs.

The sun was warm, and all the bees round the tea-trees were singing a lazy tune.

Snugglepot and Cuddlepie had been up all night and were very tired, so they fell asleep and sat hard, and all the eggs were broken. When they woke up they cried aloud, "Oh! whatever shall we do?" A big Lizard looked up from below. "What's the matter?" he asked. When they told him he only smiled.

"Why, I can get you some eggs that will do just as well," said he, and disappeared in a flash.

Presently he came back with two lovely eggs, all warm, so they put them in the nest, and the Lizard, having nothing to do, said he would ride them along their way. They chatted as they went along and soon became very good friends. By and by they entered a village. There, they were surprised to see an Editor writing all about them in his News-paper. Gumnut Editors generally write backwards, because they say it takes longer

So they both sat on the eggs

10

The Editor Writing his Leading Article

to read that way, and the people think they are getting more news.

"Why, there are our portraits," said Snugglepot.

"Oh, Mr Lizard," they cried, "please ride us away as fast as you can."

When Mr Lizard heard that they were travelling far to see a Human, he said he would like to go with them, and if they liked he would ride them all the way, for he had taken a great fancy to Snugglepot and Cuddlepie, and they already loved him; so it was agreed.

He went back to say good-bye to his wife, promising to return at once.

In the meantime Snugglepot and Cuddlepie bought two little secondhand houses from a wayside shop. (Gumnuts always carry money in their caps.)

"They will be warm to sleep in, the nights are getting cold," said Snugglepot, "and we can rest till Mr Lizard comes back."

So they settled in and both went fast asleep. In the middle of the night a spotted cat came sniffing at their houses. He had a large family to feed and had had no luck that night.

"These grubs will be better than nothing," he thought,
and was about to seize them in his mouth when a terrible noise arose above them. Scream after scream filled the night.

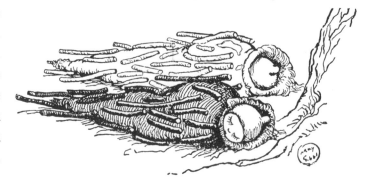

Secondhand Houses

Cuddlepie has an Idea

Snugglepot and Cuddlepie sat up. The spotted cat fled, and down the tree slid two large Native Bears. They were fighting, and as they hit each other they screamed with rage.

Snugglepot and Cuddlepie were very scared as the big Bears fought over them, then a huge foot kicked them over and they rolled down the tree to the ground. The grass was so soft and thick where they fell, and their little houses so snug, that they were not in the least hurt, only very, very frightened. They lay quite still till daybreak, and then, seeing a crowd of Nuts and Blossoms, they crawled out of their camps and went to ask questions. Everyone was talking of the horrible affair in the night.

They were fighting

The Blossom was taking her Bath

(see page 9)

The Pageant

Mrs Snake Appears

"It's the same nearly every night," said one Nut. "We get no sleep at all."

"Why not dress up and amuse them?" said Cuddlepie. "People can't be cross when they are laughing."

The Nuts and Blossoms were delighted with the idea, and everybody set about preparing their dresses.

That night, when the moon was up, they danced before the big Bears. (You can only see one in the picture—the other is higher up.) Mr and Mrs Bear were so amused that they laughed all night. Mrs Kookaburra heard the fuss and came to see what was happening. She, too, laughed all night, and the Bush rang with laughter.

When it was all over Mrs Kookaburra said she would give a big dinner party in honour of Snugglepot and Cuddlepie. They said they were delighted, but that was a polite fib, for they hated to see snakes and other dead things eaten.

Just about this time Mr Lizard returned and, hearing what was afoot, he offered to go snake-hunting for Mrs Kookaburra. "I know where there are plenty," he said, and, being a most obliging person, he went at once though he'd just been on a long journey.

By and by he came back with quite a big bag of snakes. Mrs Kookaburra was in raptures and they all sat down to dinner. Not Mr Lizard. He went to sleep.

After dinner Snugglepot and Cuddlepie went for a long walk together. On their way back a Snake popped up out of her front door and said, "Aha! where is your friend Lizard?"

"I beg your pardon," said Snugglepot.

"Who killed my Aunt and my Mother-in-law and my three Cousins?" she hissed.

"I'm afraid I don't know," answered Snugglepot.

Mrs Kookaburra's Dinner Party

"And who sat by while they were eaten?" she hissed.

"Oh, excuse me," interrupted Cuddlepie, "there's something on your lip."

"Only my breakfast," said Mrs Snake.

"Poor Mrs Snake," said Cuddlepie, "can't you afford anything but grass for your breakfast?"

"I have birds for breakfast," said Mrs Snake with dignity, "every morning."

"Oh," said Cuddlepie. "You eat birds, so birds eat you."

Mrs Snake was furious. She went green with anger and spat at them. "My next meal," she hissed, "will be boiled Lizard!" Then she drew in her wicked head and disappeared.

Snugglepot and Cuddlepie hurried to where they had left their friend asleep. He was gone. They called, but no answer came. They shouted. Still no answer.

"The Snake has got him," said Snugglepot.

"And he may be dead," said Cuddlepie.

"And being boiled," said Snugglepot. "Our dear kind Lizard. What shall we do?"

Then a voice near by called out, "Where there's a creek there's a croak."

"Who's there?" called Snugglepot. The voice said again, "Where there's a creek there's a croak."

"I know what it means," said Cuddlepie, "it means we are to ask the Frogs."

"There's a creek quite near," said Snugglepot. Then from out a bank of rushes scrambled a big-eyed Frog.

"I know the back way into Mrs Snake's house," he said, "and there in her dungeon is where you will find your friend."

Without waste of time they all hurried up the bed of the creek till they came to a deep pool where the Frogs were playing their favourite diving game. They jump in, and the one who stays longest under water wins. A little crowd had gathered to see the fun.

As they neared the pool, Mr Frog called to a friend of his. "Lanky Legs," said he, in a low voice, "these young Nuts are in trouble. A friend of theirs is a prisoner in Mrs Snake's dungeon; will you help?"

"I will," replied Lanky Legs.

"Very well," said Mr Frog, "we'll pretend to be in the game, in case Mrs Snake is watching, so you take one Nut on your back and I'll take the other. When we get under water, swim to the side and climb up through the hole that enters the cave. You know."

The Diving-Pool

Poor Mr Lizard

"I do," said Lanky Legs.

Then they mounted the high diving rock, and Cuddlepie felt very nervous. Snugglepot whispered to him, "Hold tight and hold your breath", and gave his hand a squeeze.

It was very exciting. Snugglepot went first, then Cuddlepie saw his turn had come. He shut his eyes and held tight. The Frog leapt from the rock. Splash! He felt the cold water close over him; he felt the quick movement of legs and body as Lanky

In the dungeon

Legs swam deep under the water. Then he felt himself rushing upwards and, just when his breath was all gone, they bobbed up on the surface of the water like a cork.

Cuddlepie opened his eyes. They were in a big cave. Snugglepot and Mr Frog had already landed. When they had shaken off the water and recovered their breath, Mr Frog led the way along a dark passage. Presently they came to a large opening into another cave and, looking down, they saw a sad sight. There, all bound hand and foot, limp and unconscious, with a heavy stone on his head, lay poor old Mr Lizard.

As they looked, Lanky Legs turned pale and said he must hurry back as his wife was ill. Mr Frog was made of different stuff. He went down into the dungeon with Snugglepot. Cuddlepie was left to keep watch.

When they had untied poor Mr Lizard, and rolled away the stone, he began to stir and at last opened his eyes. Snugglepot and Cuddlepie were overjoyed to see that he was alive.

"Hist!" whispered Mr Frog. They listened.

Yes, there was a noise. Some stones rattled in the far darkness of the cave.

Mr Lizard sprang up and, seizing Snugglepot, placed him on his back and dashed up and out of the cave, catching up Cuddlepie as he went. He was very much alive now.

"I know the way," he said, "hold to me."

"Oh, but where is Mr Frog?" cried Snugglepot and Cuddlepie together. "What will happen to him?" Mr Lizard stopped at once. Then they heard a faint voice calling from the distance, "Go on, I'm quite safe", so they went on.

But alas! Brave Mr Frog! He had purposely stayed behind, hopping from place to place to entice Mrs Snake to follow him instead of them, and even as he called "I'm quite safe", the great Snake caught him by his hind legs and swallowed him up.

The Hat Shop

The Hat Shop

AFTER travelling a very long way through winding passages, they came out into a pretty place all hung in green, with warm sunlight shining through.

Mr Lizard sniffed and looked about. "Why," said he, "I believe we are in the hat shop."

The Frogs' wives were very pleased
with their new hats

They peeped through a leaf curtain, and it certainly did look like a hat shop, with lots of people buying hats.

Snugglepot and Cuddlepie were charmed. "Let us buy two hats for the Frogs who helped us," said Cuddlepie. "They can give them to their wives."

"Good idea," agreed Snugglepot. So they went in and bought the two biggest hats in the shop. (You can't see them in the picture —they are in another part of the shop.)

The Cabstand

In a Large Town

When they came out into the street Snugglepot said, "What a large town!"

"It is," said Mr Lizard. "Would you like to look round while I go back with the hats?"

"Yes please," they both answered, "that will be jolly."

"I won't be long," said Mr Lizard, and he hurried away.

Snugglepot and Cuddlepie looked about. Such a lot of houses, and people, and streets! It was very bewildering.

"Why, there's a cabstand," cried Snugglepot. "Let's take a cab and drive round." So they ran to the nearest cab. It had a little

baby and looked kind. Cuddlepie went inside as he was smaller than Snugglepot, who hung on behind because there was only room for one inside. The baby stayed behind with the other cabs who promised to take care of it.

At The White City

It was a splendid ride. Snugglepot had hard work to hold on, but was enjoying himself thoroughly.

"Are there any Humans near here?" he asked the Cabbie, when they stopped for a rest.

"Why, yes," said the driver, pointing with his whip, "there's tons of 'em over there."

"Could you drive us there?" asked Snugglepot.

The Cabman shook his head. "Not safe," he replied. "They'd kill you or shut you up till you die."

A refreshment stall

Snugglepot looked at Cuddlepie. "We must see one," he said, "after coming all this way."

"Yes, but only in the distance," answered Cuddlepie.

Cuddlepie is Anxious

"Well," said the Cabman, scratching his cap, "you'd better have a good time first. Have you seen the White City?"

"No," they answered.

"You'd like that," said the Cabman.

So they got aboard the Cab again and drove on.

Snugglepot and Cuddlepie were simply in love with the White City. They had honey sticks and dew drinks at the refreshment stall. They went on the switchback over and over again. They saw the Lucky Devil dance and everything there was to see, till at last the Cab grew tired of waiting and said it must get back to its baby. (Bush Cabmen always consider their cabs, and never make them hurry if they are tired, or stand up if they want to go to sleep.)

When Snugglepot and Cuddlepie came out the Cab was gone. "Perhaps he's got another job," said Snugglepot. "Let's walk a little way; we might meet him."

As they were sauntering along they noticed a crowd of Nuts and Blossoms in the distance.

"Let's go and see," said Cuddlepie. So they went.

In the middle of a large railed-off space, upon a wonderful steed, sat a dark red-skinned Nut. He held a long stick in his hand; he sat very straight and looked very

The Lucky Devil Dance

30

On the Switchback

proud. A man wearing a long coat was walking about shouting, "Who will fight the Champion of the Red Gumnuts? Come on! Come on! Who will fight him?"

"Me!" shouted Snugglepot.

"No, no," said Cuddlepie. "You mustn't. Please, Snugglepot."

"Yes I will," said Snugglepot. And he climbed through the fence, and all the crowd shouted and clapped their hands. A large handsome Beetle steed was brought out and a long stick handed to Snugglepot. (Each stick has a pad of spider-web on the end, so that the fighters cannot hurt each other.)

Snugglepot mounted his steed and the fight began. This was the first time Snugglepot had played this game. He had not even seen it, so Cuddlepie was very anxious.

At first Snugglepot made many mistakes, and the man in the long coat had to keep shouting, "Begin again!" For there were some things not allowed in the game, such as putting the stick in the other man's eye. The game was quite simple. The man who pushed the other man off onto the ground, won the game.

The Red Nut laughed at Snugglepot, and this made him angry, so he made a great push with his stick, and off went the Red Nut's cap. The crowd grew very excited and made a great noise, for no one yet had been able to beat the Red Gumnut.

Snugglepot said to himself, "I want to beat him, and I will." Then he found to his joy that he was getting on splendidly; his Beetle liked him and was helping him. When Snugglepot pushed against the Red Nut, the Beetle rose on his six legs and pushed too. When the Red Nut pushed *his* stick upon Snugglepot, the clever Beetle backed and backed, and all the time the Red Nut's handsome Beetle was standing quite still.

A Strange Thing Happens

Snugglepot thought this wasn't fair to the Red Nut, so he said to his own Beetle, "Go close up and stand firm." The Beetle went up close and stood firm, then Snugglepot gave a great shout and a great push, and off went the Red Nut plump on to the ground.

The Red Nut picked himself up and shook hands with Snugglepot, and the Nuts and Blossoms crowded round him saying how strong he was, and then in the middle of it all a strange thing happened. Someone pushed through the crowd, weeping bitterly. It was Mrs Fantail, and close beside her came two large baby lizards.

"Oh!" she cried, when she saw Snugglepot, "see what hatched out of the eggs you nursed for me. They won't leave me—they will hold on to my wings—I can't fly—I'm so miserable."

"Snugglepot," said Cuddlepie, "we'd better tell about——"

"What?" said all the crowd, who were listening.

"Please go away," said Cuddlepie, "it's only Mrs Fantail who ought to hear."

Mr Lizard is Upset

In the Bush everyone is polite when they are asked to be, so all the Nuts and Blossoms and the Red Nut went away at once. Then Snugglepot and Cuddlepie told Mrs Fantail about the broken eggs, and how kind Mr Lizard had been.

Poor Mrs Fantail simply screamed when she heard. But when Snugglepot said he would ask Mr Lizard to take the young ones back to their own home, she stopped crying. Then both the young Lizards began to howl. They said they didn't want to go; they wanted to stay with their little mother. This was awkward. Snugglepot and Cuddlepie got redder and redder. They felt so ashamed of all the trouble they had brought to poor Mrs Fantail.

"I'll tell you what," said Snugglepot. "You stay here, please, Mrs Fantail, and we'll go and find Mr Lizard." And he and Cuddlepie ran off, feeling very glad to be away by themselves where they could talk about it all.

After hunting for a while they found Mr Lizard at the photographers. When they told him what had happened, he turned so pale that the photographer said, quite crossly, "If you look so white, you won't come out at all." But when they told how the young Lizards wouldn't leave Mrs Fantail, Mr Lizard was very upset, and his tail began to tremble.

The photographer popped out from under his hood. "You'll have three tails in the picture if you twitch about like that," he said, very angry. But Mr Lizard was too upset to stand still any longer. "Excuse me," he said, and rushed out of the place.

Snugglepot and Cuddlepie found him outside kicking the wall and saying, "Gum it all! Gum it all! What a fool I am!"

"Why?" asked Cuddlepie.

"Because I don't know whose house I took the eggs from, so how can I take them home?"

They Found Mr Lizard at the Photographer's

The Dance

This was most awkward.

"Oh, I know what," cried Cuddlepie.

"What?" asked the other two, breathlessly.

"You can adopt them, Mr Lizard," said Cuddlepie.

"Of course," said Snugglepot.

"But what will my wife say?" said Mr Lizard.

"Oh, well," said Cuddlepie, "you won't know that till you get home."

"But I can guess," muttered Mr Lizard.

When they said good-bye to Mrs Fantail, who flew happily home, and had seen Mr Lizard off with his two adopted children sitting on his back, Snugglepot and Cuddlepie heaved a sigh of relief.

"What shall we do now?" said Snugglepot.

"Nothing," said Cuddlepie.

"That's a good idea," said Snugglepot; so they sat down in the lacy shadow of a Boronia bush and soon fell fast asleep.

They woke to the sound of gay music. A band was playing quite near, birds were singing, frogs croaking, cicadas and crickets and bees, and a little brook, all were in the band. It was a rag-time, and Snugglepot and Cuddlepie grew restless. They heard voices.

"They are inside this wall," said Cuddlepie. "Here's a crack; let's look in." So they peeped, and there they saw a jolly party, all dancing very hard, as if they were in a great hurry but had nowhere to go. Quite near to them, Snugglepot and Cuddlepie saw a poor little Blossom sitting all alone. Her dress was torn, and she was very dirty and sad—nobody danced with her.

"I'll get in," said Snugglepot, "and ask her to dance."

Better No Clothes than No Manners

So he crawled through the crack when no one was looking and asked the little Blossom to dance with him. The little girl was so pleased.

Now, Snugglepot couldn't dance, and the little girl couldn't dance, so they got in everybody's way, and everybody looked crossly at them. Then they heard someone say, "What a dirty little Blossom, and the Nut has no clothes on. They ought not to be allowed in."

Snugglepot was filled with pity for the poor little girl. "I'm sorry I've no clothes," he said. "Where I come from they don't wear any."

"That doesn't matter," said little Ragged Blossom. "It's better to be a kind Nut with no clothes than an unkind one all dressed up."

"But I'd like to get some," said Snugglepot.

"My uncle sells very cheap ones," said Ragged Blossom. "Shall I show you his shop?"

"Yes, please," said Snugglepot.

In his anxiety to buy clothes he forgot all about poor Cuddlepie, and they went out of the dancing-hall by another way. So Cuddlepie waited and waited and waited, till he grew tired and fell asleep again.

While he was asleep he had a dream. He thought someone was calling him, so he got up and followed the voice; and he really did get up and walk along, though he was fast asleep all the time.

Her Uncle's Shop

The Terrible Trap

Cuddlepie Walks in His Sleep

"Cuddlepie, come here!" the voice kept calling, and, as it called, Cuddlepie followed, with eyes wide open, yet fast asleep, till by and by he came to a little stream. When his foot touched the water, he woke up.

"Help me, help me," called a faint voice near him.

"Where are you?" called Cuddlepie.

"I'm here. Help me," came the voice more faintly.

Cuddlepie scrambled, and pushed, and tore his way through the sticks, and leaves, and ferns till he came to an open space at the foot of a big tree. Then he stood in horror. He saw a terrible thing. A great iron trap was there, chained to a stake, and tightly shut were its great iron teeth—shut upon the arm of a poor grey Possum. Tears were running down his face, and the big, gentle brown eyes looked at Cuddlepie in an agony of pain.

"Oh! poor dear Possum! Who did this to you?" asked Cuddlepie.

"Humans," said the Possum. "They set these traps at our very doors and we run into them before we see them."

Cuddlepie was too unhappy to speak. He went to the stream and brought back some water in his cap, but the Possum was quite still and his eyes were shut.

"Oh!" said Cuddlepie in anguish, "Possum, dear Possum, don't say you're dead!" But the Possum lay quite still.

Many an Uncle is No Relation

ALL this time Snugglepot was in the Uncle's shop trying on clothes. There were strings of them hanging up, and some spiders and grubs sat on a high place, hard at work, making and mending. Snugglepot was very excited.

"This is my first pair," he said.

"You look fine," said the Uncle. "They fit like a cocoon."

So Snugglepot bought that suit, and a nice walking-stick also. When he came out looking so grand, little Ragged Blossom felt quite shy. She hid her face under her shabby hat, and said, "I liked the dance and I like you; I'm going home now", and ran away.

Snugglepot was surprised. He couldn't say anything; and, when at last he thought of running after her, she had disappeared. But little Ragged Blossom didn't go home—she had none to go to. She was just a little orphan. The Bush creatures were kind to her, but she was nobody's business, and she had no one to love her.

Suddenly Snugglepot remembered Cuddlepie. He thought he heard his voice calling in the distance.

It was Cuddlepie.

When he had seen the poor Possum lying so still, he had grown frightened, and shouted, "Help! Help!! Help!!!" And he shouted louder and louder, till Snugglepot heard him and coo-eed back and came hurrying to find him, while little Ragged Blossom, who was hiding, crept out and came after him. A lot of Bush creatures were running in the same direction, and quite a crowd had gathered by the time Snugglepot reached the place.

When Cuddlepie saw Snugglepot he burst into tears, and cried, "See! Oh, see what the Humans have done."

The Pity of It

Snugglepot was filled with grief and the tears ran down his cheeks, while all the Bush creatures cried in their own way. Nothing could be done. No one was strong enough to open the great trap. The poor, gentle Possum must stay there till he died.

Now, as everyone stood there weeping for pity, a great noise came sounding on the breeze. All the Bush creatures turned pale. "Humans! Humans!" they cried, and scuttled away, tumbling over each other in their haste to hide.

Snugglepot and Cuddlepie stood spellbound as the great noise came nearer. Then little Ragged Blossom ran to Snugglepot. "Come, hide quickly!" she cried, and led them up the Possum track to a cave in the side of the tree.

Just as they reached it a monster Dog came crashing through the Bush and stood over the trap barking, while close behind him came a monster Human.

"Why, it looks like a giant nut," said Snugglepot, "and he's got eyes like ours."

"Look! what's he doing?" whispered Cuddlepie. "Oh! Oh! he's going to kill the poor Possum."

But no! The monster Human opened the trap with his strong hands and gently lifted out the little Possum. Then he bound up the poor broken leg, and they heard him say, "These rotten traps, I hate them." And he pulled up the stake and flung the trap into the stream. Then he said, "Come on", to the monster Dog, and they both walked away through the Bush.

Snugglepot and Cuddlepie and Little Blossom were amazed. When all sounds of the monsters had died away, they hurried down to the Possum. His eyes were open, and he gladly drank some water. Soon he was so much better that they helped him home.

"Well," said Snugglepot, when they were at last on the road again by themselves. (Ragged Blossom had stayed to help Mr Possum.) "Well!" he said, "we have seen a Human."

"Yes," said Cuddlepie.

"And a kind one, too," said Snugglepot.

"I wish," said Cuddlepie, "that all Humans were kind to Bush creatures like that."

As they went along, Cuddlepie noticed Snugglepot's new suit and stick. "Oh! Snugglepot!" he exclaimed, "what's the matter with you?"

"I'm dressed," said Snugglepot. "Everybody does it here."

Lilly Pilly's Bull-dog

"Oh," said Cuddlepie, quite bewildered, "must I wear those flappy things, too?"

"Of course, and we'll go and get them now," said Snugglepot.

So they went back to the Uncle's and bought a nice suit for Cuddlepie, and they both went strutting down the street, feeling most important.

By this time it was getting dark, and all the glow worms were alight in the shop windows. As they were looking at the beautiful window of Cob Web & Co., a pretty girl passed them. Snugglepot was glad he had on his new clothes and walking-stick.

It was Lilly Pilly, the actress, with her favourite Bull-dog Ant. She looked at Snugglepot and Cuddlepie, and they looked at her.

Cuddlepie said, "What a splendid Bull-dog!" and then they all smiled and patted the Bull-dog; but the Bull-dog, who didn't like being patted by strangers, caught hold of the tail of Snugglepot's new suit and held on. Cuddlepie caught hold of the Bull-dog's tail and pulled, and Lilly Pilly caught Cuddlepie round the waist and she pulled; then Snugglepot, to keep himself from falling, held on to a post. Then they all pulled, and the tail of Snugglepot's new suit tore, and everybody went down, just as Mr Lizard came running round the corner; so they all fell against him and knocked him over, and he went rolling down the hill into Mrs Busy Blossom's washing day, and there *was* a mess.

As all this was happening, Lilly Pilly's father drove up. He was a fat sort of person, who always ate too much and had a lot of money. He was so amused to see them all go down that he laughed till he cried, and said, "I'll have that in my new Picture Play, and you must be the actors." He shook hands with Snuggle-

Snugglepot and Cuddlepie Meet Lilly Pilly

pot and Cuddlepie, and gave them tickets for the Picture Show. Then he drove away, taking Lilly Pilly and the Bull-dog with him. He didn't look quite the right shape to be the father of Lilly Pilly, but it's often so in life.

Mr Lizard wasn't really hurt; only a little upset. Snugglepot and Cuddlepie were so pleased to see him back, and they all went off to the Uncle's shop to get Snugglepot's suit mended.

When Mr Pilly had handed the tickets to Snugglepot, he had dropped one, and little Ragged Blossom, coming along soon after, found it. She could hardly believe it was real, and shouted with joy

In the Park

A Wicked Thief

—so loudly that wicked Mrs Snake, who had been following Mr Lizard, crept out, and was just in time to see her put the precious ticket in her hat.

Mrs Snake rustled her scales and flicked her tongue in glee, as she slid along after little Ragged Blossom. It was quite dark now, and Blossom was hungry and tired; but she was happy, for she was going to the Pictures at last.

Mrs Snake followed her all the way to a park, and saw her wrap herself in a big leaf and curl up in the corner of an old seat. Just as dogs can smell all sorts of things that Humans can't, so to the Nuts and Blossoms even the smallest flower has its scent. Ragged Blossom slept on the broken seat because she liked the scent of the mauve orchid.

When she was quite fast asleep Mrs Snake crept up and very slyly stole the ticket. Poor little Blossom woke just too late. She thought in her dream that someone was giving her a splendid new hat, and when she opened her eyes she saw the shining tail of Mrs Snake slipping away among the ferns. She felt in her hat. The ticket was gone!

Only just in time she remembered not to scream—for Ragged Blossom was a kind little girl, and knew that some poor ladies were asleep on the next seat, and she didn't want to wake them. Hurrying through the ferns softly, she was in time to see Mrs Snake disappearing into a hole.

Blossom followed. It was very dark, and she was afraid; but the ticket—she must get it. Presently she saw a light at the end of the passage, and, creeping up very carefully, she listened.

And a Wicked Plot

She heard the loud voices of Mrs Snake's friends, the wicked Banksia men.

One said, "They'll be at the Lilly Pilly Pictures tomorrow; the Lizard will be outside. We must steal the Nuts and keep them till the Lizard comes to look for them, then we'll only give them up in exchange for him."

"Aha!" said Mrs Snake's voice, "that'll get him, the monster! How I hate him!"

"We'll starve those fat Nuts," said one angry voice.

"Do 'em good," said another horrible voice.

"And we'll kill the ugly Lizard they're so fond of," said Mrs Snake's awful voice.

When Blossom heard these terrible things her hair stood straight up with fright. It was very cold in the passage, and, before she could stop it, Blossom sneezed. Mrs Snake darted to the door, and was so astonished to see Blossom that she stood still, staring. Little Blossom sank trembling to the ground, her hands in the dust. Suddenly she thought of something. Like a flash she dashed two handfuls of dust into Mrs Snake's eyes, then jumped up and ran. It was uphill, but she ran. She was breathless, but she ran and ran. Her knees were giving way, but still she ran. She could hear them coming. Faster she ran, until at last she came to the top and fell out upon the moss.

They were coming! they were close behind! Blossom had just strength enough to crawl under a dead gum leaf and lie there as still as the moss. Several Banksia men came hurrying out of the hole.

"She's not out here," said one.

"She must have hidden in the passage," said another.

"Perhaps she's under that leaf," said a third.

Blossom nearly jumped, but held her breath.

"What was that?" said one.

"It's Mrs Snake; she must have found her. Come on." Then they all went in again, and Blossom heard them running and shouting down under the ground.

Worn out with excitement and running, Little Blossom sank into a long sleep. She was awakened by the heavy tread of a big Grey Possum on his rounds. (They are the policemen at night time because they can see in the dark.)

"Sh! Sh! What are you doing?" he asked, and Ragged Blossom told him everything.

"I'll watch the door while you go and warn the Nuts," said

he. "I'd go with you only it's getting light; I'll soon have to go to bed."

"Yes, it is," said Blossom, "I can hear the Ants taking round the Aphis milk." So she hurried away.

It was nearly sunrise by the time she reached the city. Already it was getting warm, and the air was full of nice noises and sweet scents; the streets were crowded; busy Ants were running about everywhere; Beetle carts were labouring along; gay Nuts and fresh Blossoms were walking and chatting; Woodcutters were at work in the dark, everyone seemed busy and happy.

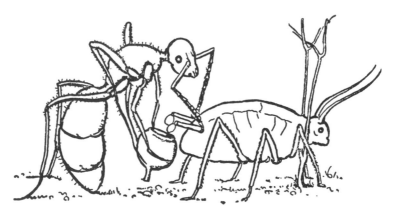

Milking the Aphis

Poor Little Blossom was worried and sad. Who would listen to her story? She was so little and ragged. She must do something all by herself, but what could she do? She thought very hard, and soon a plan came to her.

She looked into lots of backyards till she saw a long spider-web clothes line; and, as it was not washing-day, she borrowed it. Then she hurried along to the Lilly Pilly Picture Palace.

Tears fell as she thought of her beautiful ticket; but she was not a cry-baby, so she wiped away her tears and got to work.

First she climbed right up onto the top of the high building. It took a long time. Then she made a hole in the roof and tied one

The Lilly Pilly Picture Palace

end of the rope firmly to a beam. No one noticed her, she was only like a fly on the roof. It was terrible to have to wait so long, but at last the people came. From her high perch she watched them crowd in; and at last, looking through the hole in the roof, she saw Snugglepot and Cuddlepie. There they were almost underneath her, near the wall. It was nearly time for the show to begin.

Kind old Mr Lizard was dozing out in the sun; and, behind him, in the deep shadows, she could see the glistening, wicked eyes of Mrs Snake and the bushy heads of the bad Banksia men.

Little Blossom longed to call to Mr Lizard and wake him; but she knew that would only warn the wicked ones, and they would then go away and make another plot; so she kept still and waited.

Presently the lights went out, and now was the time. A wonderful picture was showing. It was the Funny Nut, and every one was screaming with laughter. This was the very moment. Quickly she let down the rope till it hung just above the heads of Snugglepot and Cuddlepie; then she slid down beside Snugglepot. "Hush!" she whispered, "please let me see the pictures instead of you. I've never seen any; please do!"

Snugglepot and Cuddlepie were most astonished, but they had good bush manners, so Snugglepot only said, "Of course, you take my place and I'll go out."

"No, let me," whispered Cuddlepie.

At the Picture Show

Caught!

"No, I will," answered Snugglepot, and he began to climb the rope. Cuddlepie followed, to argue with him, and they went up higher and higher still, saying, "I want to go"—"No, I will", and all the time the people were shouting with laughter at the picture and didn't see or hear them.

Little Ragged Blossom looked up; Snugglepot and Cuddlepie were safely out on the roof. She wanted to follow, but was too frightened.

Through the darkness she saw the wicked eyes of a Banksia man looking at her. Then something dashed in, grabbed her by the legs, dragged her out of the seat, hoisted her over the heads of the people and out of the Picture Show, all in a moment, faster than it can be told.

A hand was over her mouth, so she couldn't scream. She was carried along at a great speed, then she heard shouting and a great noise of people racing after them. "Stop them! Stop them!" they were calling. At last they came to a steep hill.

"Throw her down," hissed Mrs Snake.

"Not me," panted the angry Banksia man.

Then quite suddenly they all seemed to fall down a big hole, and they rolled and rolled till they came to the bottom, and lay there panting.

"Thank goodness we're home," said Mrs Snake, as soon as she got her breath again. "Tie her up, and come and get something to drink." But Little Blossom couldn't run now, she lay quite still and cold.

"Never mind her, she's dead," said a Banksia man.

"We'll get into trouble if she is," said another.

"Pooh! She's only a little stray; no one will miss her", and so saying, Mrs Snake and the wicked Banksia men went away.

A Knowing Tramp

IT was late in the afternoon, and Snugglepot and Cuddlepie and Mr Lizard were chewing wattle gum and resting by the road-side.

"How did you get up there on the roof?" asked Mr Lizard. Snugglepot told him.

"Why!" exclaimed Mr Lizard, "she must have known the plot and was trying to save you."

"Poor kind little Blossom," said Snugglepot, "if only we could find her!"

"Let's ask this tramp if he's seen them," said Cuddlepie, as a tramp came hobbling along the road.

"Well, yes," he said, rubbing his bushy beard, "I seen some nasty-lookin' folk runnin' away with a little girl. They went in that direction. I heard 'em say they was goin' to the Gum Inn."

"The Gum Inn," shouted Mr Lizard. "Jump on, we'll soon have them!"

As they galloped away, the old tramp threw back his head and laughed. He wasn't a tramp at all, but one of the wicked Banksia men disguised in a paperbark cloak. He hurried back to Mrs Snake.

"It's all right," he said, "I've sent them to the Gum Inn. If we hurry by the underground passage we'll get there first."

"Good man," said Mrs Snake.

Little Blossom, lying still, heard all that was said.

"What shall we do with her?" asked the Banksia men.

"Take her as far as the dungeon and throw her in. She's dead, or if not she soon will be," said wicked Mrs Snake.

"Right-o," said all the bad men.

So they picked up little Blossom and all started off. Blossom pretended to be dead, and, when they left her in the dungeon, lay still long after they had gone and their steps had died away. As she lay there, afraid to move, she heard a scratching noise quite near, and presently, in the dim light of the cave, she saw the earth and stones moving. Then a big hand came out of the earth, then another hand, then a face and two big eyes.

"Who are you?" said the face.

"I'm only little Ragged Blossom," said the poor little thing. "Please, don't kill me, please don't."

"Are you a friend of Mrs Snake?" asked the face.

"No, I hate her," said Ragged Blossom, who was always truthful.

"So do I," said the face, and then the earth and stones heaved and out stepped a big Frog. He was very thin and pale, and seemed weak.

"Don't be afraid of me," he said kindly; and he patted Blossom so gently that she burst into tears and told him all the story about Mrs Snake trying to catch Snugglepot and Cuddlepie, and how she meant to kill poor Mr Lizard. When the Frog heard this he grew very angry.

"Now is our chance to escape," he said; "they have left the door of the dungeon open. Come, I know the way to the river. Quick! I'll carry you;" and the big Frog carried little Blossom till they came to a cave with a lake in it.

"Shut your eyes and hold on to me, and don't be afraid," said the Frog, and then he dived into the water and swam under, and came out into the diving-pool. Mr Frog clambered out and looked round. No one was about.

"Come," said he, shaking the water off little Blossom. "Quickly! There's no time to lose."

He hurried down the bed of the creek till they came to a big river. Here, under the rushes, lay a little boat. They jumped in. He pushed out into the stream and away they went, twirling and

The little boat was called "The Kurrajong"

bobbing along with the current. After rushing down the stream at a great rate for some time, Mr Frog guided the little boat into a quiet pool and pushed her on to the bank.

"Where are we?" asked Blossom.

"In the garden of the Gum Inn," he answered.

The Nut on the Sign

"Come on! Hurry! or we shall be too late," he cried; and, as he spoke, a loud shriek filled the air; then shouts and more shrieks. Mr Frog turned pale, and Blossom's knees shook so that she could scarcely run. All the time, as they hurried up through the garden, they could hear the terrible noise.

"They must be killing . . ." began Blossom.

"Don't talk; hurry!" said the Frog; and he went so fast that she could scarcely keep him in sight. At the top of the garden was a little gateway leading into the road. They opened it and looked out.

What they saw made them stand rooted to the spot with horror. There, in front of the Inn, riding on the Lizard, were Snugglepot and Cuddlepie. Mr Lizard was reared up on his hind legs, and there, almost upon them, was the huge shining body of Mrs Snake. Her head was raised to strike; but now a wonderful thing happened.

High above Mrs Snake swung the sign of the Gum Inn, and on it sat a Nut painting it, who, seeing what was about to happen, sprang from the sign right upon the neck of Mrs Snake, and, with arms and legs about her throat, held her fast.

Her great tail whipped the road. Everyone screamed. The Lizard dashed upon her, and held her down. Snugglepot and Cuddlepie shouted to some men who all rushed upon her. More men came running down the road, and men from the Inn. Mr Frog came to himself and leapt upon her. With so many against her, Mrs Snake saw that her end had come. She called, "Help! Friends, help!" But the cowardly Banksia men had fled, and were now far away.

So Mrs Snake was tied head and tail till she couldn't move, and her wicked head was knocked off. A great shout went up, for she was very wicked and deserved to die, and everyone was glad.

The Gum Inn

The Big Thin Frog

Then Lilly Pilly's father asked everybody to a grand dinner at the Gum Inn, and just then Snugglepot and Cuddlepie saw the big, thin Frog.

"Why," they exclaimed, shaking his hands, "where have you come from?"

"From inside that Snake," said Mr Frog. "When you left the dungeon she swallowed me; but when she went to sleep I scratched her throat and she coughed, so I jumped out and have lain hidden there ever since."

Everyone thought this the most wonderful story they had ever heard.

"But where is the little girl?" said Mr Frog.

"What little girl?" asked Lilly Pilly.

"The little ragged girl," said Mr Frog, "who was with me just a moment ago."

When Snugglepot and Cuddlepie heard this they rushed out and found poor little Blossom, who was just turning away because she felt so dirty.

"Why," said Lilly Pilly, who came hurrying after Snugglepot and Cuddlepie, "she's just the very one for Father's new Picture Play." Then she kissed little Ragged Blossom and asked her to come to the great dinner.

"I'll give you a new frock, and you shall come with me, and live in my home, and be my little sister—I haven't any mother or sisters," said Lilly Pilly.

Little Ragged Blossom was too happy to speak. Mr Pilly patted her kindly and gave everyone a ticket for the Gum Blossom Ballet, which was to begin at his big theatre that very night. Everybody gave three cheers for Mr Pilly and Lilly Pilly, and some more cheers

Everyone Happy

for Ragged Blossom; then cheers for Snugglepot and Cuddlepie and
Mr Lizard, and then a lot more noise for themselves because they
were so happy.

.   .   .   .

Here is the end of this book.

Snugglepot and Cuddlepie had many more adventures. I may
tell you about them some day.

Little Ragged Blossom

Further Adventures of Ragged Blossom, Snugglepot and Cuddlepie

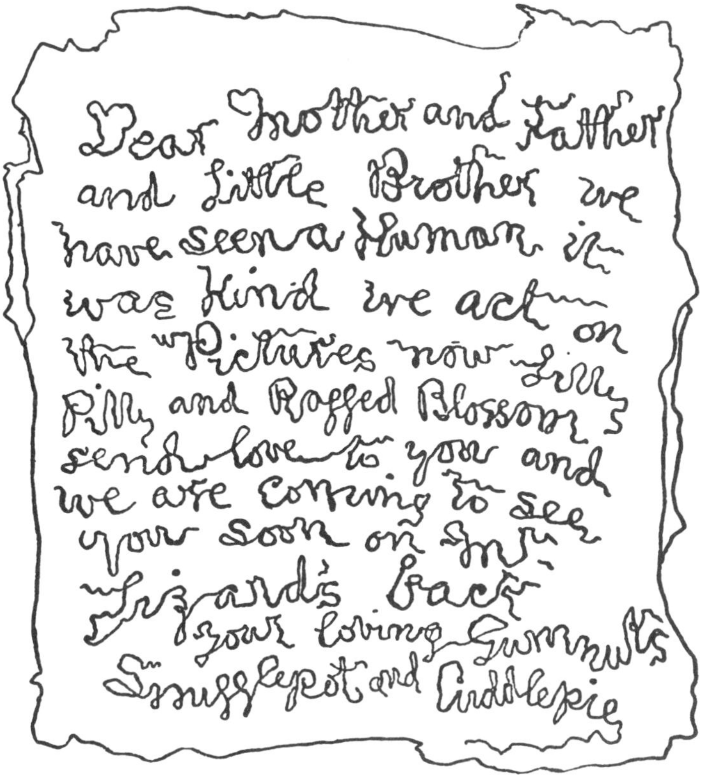

Dear Mother and Father
and little Brother we
have seen a Human it
was kind we act on
the "Pictures now Lilly
Pilly and Ragged Blossom's
send love to you and
we are coming to see
you soon on a
Lizard's back
Your loving Gumnuts
Snugglepot and Cuddlepie

Snugglepot and Cuddlepie wrote this letter on
paperbark and sent it home by bird post

Little Ragged Blossom

(AND MORE ABOUT SNUGGLEPOT AND CUDDLEPIE)

You remember how, upon the killing of wicked Mrs Snake, every-one became joyful, and rich Mr Pilly, the father of Lilly Pilly the actress, gave a dinner party at the Gum Inn; and how, afterwards, everyone was given a ticket for the Gum Blossom Ballet at Mr Pilly's new Theatre.

Very well then.

Now, when the bad Banksia men saw their friend Mrs Snake being overpowered by the Gumnuts, and Mr Lizard, and Mr Frog, and their friends, they grew afraid and fled, and when they had come to their safe hiding-place they drew together in council to see how they might plan to revenge themselves on Snugglepot and Cuddlepie and Ragged Blossom.

"For," they said, "if we destroy these stupid Nuts, their friend Mr Lizard will die of anguish, and he is our greatest enemy."

"Our hated foe," said one.

"Smoke and burn him," growled another.

"Drop and drown him," snarled another.

"Ha," said the biggest Banksia man, "that's a good idea. We'll drown them. Ha! Ha! Listen."

Then all the bad Banksia men put their heads together and made a wicked plot.

"Greedy"

Now it happened that just under the tree where they were sitting hidden by a bush lay a friend of Mr Lizard. When he heard Mr Lizard's name he cocked his head and listened, and when he heard what they said about drowning the Nuts he crept softly away till he was out of sight; then he dashed along as fast as he could to find Mr Lizard and tell him.

But alas! his warning was never given. Just hear what comes of being greedy. Many people, when they go to big dinner parties, eat and drink more than is good for them—because the things are good and they are greedy.

Mr Lizard lay moaning

Mr Lizard was one of those "Greedies". He ate and drank so much at Mr Pilly's party that he had to stay in bed all the next day; and his head ached, and the flies worried him, and he was so cross that no one could go near him; so when he saw his friend coming he shouted, "Go away! I'm sick! Go away!" And he lashed his tail and wouldn't listen to a word. Naturally his friend was offended and went away.

So it happened that, while Mr Lizard lay moaning and groaning, all sorts of things were afoot and he knew nothing about them.

The Banksia Men Make a Wicked Plot

Alas! too Late

A big ship was lying in the harbour, and the Captain had come ashore, and had invited Ragged Blossom and Snugglepot and Cuddlepie to go on a long journey with him, and see new countries.

Quite a lot of other Nuts and Blossoms said they would like to go too, so it was arranged that *The Snag* should sail at once, and everybody was busy packing; and all the time Mr Lizard lay tossing and grumbling on his bed.

Now, in their excitement, Snugglepot and Cuddlepie forgot all about Mr Lizard; and it was not until the ship was towing out into the stream that Mr Lizard, hearing the shouts of the crowd on the wharf, sprang out of bed and rushed wildly down, calling, "Stop! Stop! Wait for me!"

All the crowd took up the cry and shouted, "Stop!"

Snugglepot and Cuddlepie saw Mr Lizard and ran to the Captain, begging him to put back. But the Captain, who was a big stern man with a great beard and bushy eyebrows, frowned at them, and said, "The tide's going out and we must go with it."

Then were Snugglepot and Cuddlepie very sad, and Ragged Blossom dropped tears into the sea as she hung over the side waving to poor Mr Lizard.

"Oh, why did we forget him?" moaned Snugglepot.

"He was so kind to me," wailed Ragged Blossom.

"Our dear old friend," sobbed Cuddlepie.

Mr Lizard, frantic with distress, jumped into a little boat and rowed after them. He pulled with all his might, and the Nuts on the ship shouted, "Come on!" The people on the wharf shouted "Hurrah!" as they saw his little boat get nearer and nearer to the big ship.

But alas! just as he was nearly touching the side the breeze caught the big green sails, filling them, and away went *The Snag*

The Sailing of The Snag

out to sea, leaving Mr Lizard in his little boat far behind, like a speck in the distance. Mr Lizard sat stiff as a tree trunk, staring after *The Snag*; his eyes looked as if they would pop out, and he ground his teeth with rage.

"Oh, Gum! Gum! Gum!" he groaned. Then he fell in a heap and rocked the boat in his grief and anger, for he had seen the Captain and he knew!

That big Captain, with his scrubby beard and bushy eyebrows, was—who do you think? He was the biggest and baddest of the Banksia men. "And no one knows," cried Mr Lizard.

The air was fresh, and the little waves danced and sparkled in the sun as *The Snag* sailed gracefully on, looking very like a big green butterfly on a blue sea.

Everybody walked up and down the decks, laughing and chatting.

Snugglepot and Cuddlepie and Ragged Blossom walked up and down too, and it was all so exciting and lovely that they soon forgot poor Mr Lizard again.

Begging him to put back

Now, though they didn't notice it, the little waves were growing bigger all the time, and the wind was getting stronger.

"Isn't it gummy!" said Ragged Blossom.

Ups and Downs

"Tree top!" cried Cuddlepie.

"Juicy!" chuckled Snugglepot.

And all the time the waves were getting bigger and bigger.

"Look at all those people leaning over the side. I wonder what they're looking at?" said Cuddlepie.

"Oh!" said Snugglepot, "I feel strange!"

"So do I," said Ragged Blossom.

"I've got a pain in my belt," groaned Cuddlepie.

"I feel stranger and stranger," said Snugglepot.

"I think I'll go to bunk," said Ragged Blossom.

But just then *The Snag* rose up over a huge wave, and they all sat down and slid along the deck; then *The Snag* rose up at the other end and they all slid back again.

"I don't like it," said Ragged Blossom.

"I hate it," said Snugglepot.

"So do I," said Cuddlepie.

Then *The Snag* rolled on one side and they all slid that way;

They all slid back again

75

In the Dark

then she rolled to the other side and they all slid the other way; but this time they all went flop, bump, into a deep dark hold and landed upon a lot of feathers.

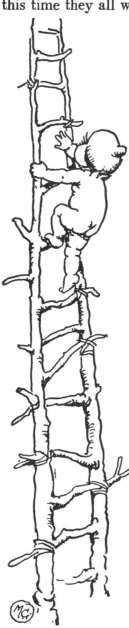

"Where are we?" said Cuddlepie.

"In the bottom of the boat, I think," said Snugglepot.

"Hush," whispered Ragged Blossom, "I can hear voices."

They all kept very still and listened; and some way off, in the darkness, they heard the Captain's voice.

"Now mind!" he was saying, "No nonsense. As soon as the moon is gone and the dark nights come, over they go—all three of 'em—twig?"

"Ay, Ay! Sir," said a gruff voice.

"You do your work quickly," said the Captain, "and I'll see you get paid well, and—dumb's the word—twig?"

"Ay, Ay! Sir," answered the gruff voice.

The Nuts held their breath. They knew now who the Captain was, and they knew he meant them to be thrown into the sea when the dark nights came.

Then the Captain and the sailor climbed up out of the hold by a long ladder, and went away.

"It's the Banksia man," whispered Snugglepot.

"What shall we do?" asked Ragged Blossom.

"It's bright moonlight tonight," said Snugglepot, "so we are safe."

Up the long ladder   76

Jerboa

"Let's hide in one of those big empty nuts," said Cuddlepie.

"Oh! good root!" said Snugglepot. "And I'll go and bring down some food."

"Do be careful no one sees you," said Ragged Blossom.

"I'll be cunning as a dingo," said Snugglepot, and off he went up the long ladder, for he was very brave.

By this time Cuddlepie and Ragged Blossom had grown used to the dark hold, and could see quite a lot of things around them.

There were passengers' trunks and bags, and a stack of huge nuts.

Now, as they crept about, they heard a noise behind some bundles of clothes-props.

"What was that?" whispered Ragged Blossom.

"I don't know, I'll go and see," said Cuddlepie.

"Oh! Look! Look!" exclaimed Ragged Blossom, and there, quite close to them, sticking out of a crack, was the end of a grey tail.

Cuddlepie seized it and pulled.

But the owner of the tail held fast.

"Come out," cried Cuddlepie, "or I'll pull your tail off."

"Oh! Oh!" squeaked a little voice. "Let me go, and I'll come out."

"Very well, quicksticks," said Cuddlepie, and out crept a thin pale little rat, with big frightened eyes and nervous whiskers.

Little Jerboa

The Escape

"What's your name?" asked Cuddlepie.

"Jerboa," said the poor little chap. "But they mostly call me Winky."

"You're a stowaway?" said Cuddlepie. "Yes, Sir," answered Winky.

"Where are you going?" asked Cuddlepie.

"Back to my mother please, Sir," said the poor little fellow, with tears in his eyes. "I ran away from home to look for raisins, and I lost myself, I did, and I had an unhappy time, Sir. Snakes nearly ate me, and owls nearly ate me, and the Banksia men beat me; and I hid aboard this ship, when I heard them say it was bound for Big Bad City, and I want to go home to my mother, I do; and I'm so hungry and cold I am, Sir; please don't tell the Captain."

"Poor little man," said Ragged Blossom. "We'll give you some food when Snugglepot comes."

"I won't tell," said Cuddlepie, and he sat down by Winky and told him all about how the bad Captain wanted to drown them. "So, you see, we must hide down here too, and we'll all help each other."

"Well," said little Jerboa eagerly, "we shall get to Big Bad tonight, and I can show you a way off the ship."

"Oh, can you?" said Cuddlepie and Ragged Blossom. "How kind of you!"

And, as they were talking, here came Snugglepot, climbing down the long ladder in great haste.

"We're nearly into a city, and—" then seeing Jerboa, he stopped in amazement.

"He's a friend," said Cuddlepie, and he told Snugglepot all the news.

"Oh! good root!" said Snugglepot. "Now we'll eat some tips and things. I got them from the cook."

By this time the evening was closing in, and night fell upon the ship, and it became very dark; and presently, when the ship was tied to the wharf and everybody was bustling about, they all crept out of the hold, led by Jerboa, and along the deck in the shadow of the side.

Once they were nearly discovered.

A funny old woman, who was running about looking for her luggage, tripped upon the end of Jerboa's long tail; she screamed, but there was so much noise and bustle that no one took any notice, and they crept on along the deck till they came to a place where a big rope was tied, stretched tightly from the ship's side across to the wharf.

"Now," said Winky, "this is the way. Cling to me and I'll take you over one at a time."

When they were safely landed on the wharf, Winky said, "Follow me as fast as you can", and he ran off into a dark shed, and they all ran after him.

It was a long run—over fences, down roads, across bridges, through gardens, over roofs, till at last everyone was tired out and it was getting light and all the birds were talking.

So they rested and looked about them. They were in a broad road with large houses on each side. Presently the sun rose and, as they sat warming, there came a large crowd of Nuts down the road, holding up flags, and singing.

"It's a Strike procession," explained Winky.

"How? What?" asked Snugglepot.

"It's a new way of making money," said Winky. "Everybody strikes in Big Bad, and the one who hits the hardest gets the most."

"Bully Ant!" said Snugglepot, "and who gets hit?"

"Everybody," said Winky.

"Let's go away then," said Ragged Blossom.

"It's only a little way to my home," said Winky, and he led them down a lane to a dear little house all made of branches.

Poor Winky! There was a note on the door to say they were all away looking for him. He wept bitterly.

The Gumnut Strike

Three Ways

"Never mind," said Ragged Blossom, "you stay here and keep the house clean, and, when they come home, how pleased they'll be!"

So Winky cheered up, and showed them over his home.

It was full of rooms, all leading out of passages, and the rooms were lined with grass.

"Stay with me," said Winky, "till you get a home of your own."

"Thank you, dear Winky," they all said. "And now we'll all go out looking for work and make some money."

"There's plenty of work," said Winky.

So Snugglepot went one way, and Cuddlepie another way, and Ragged Blossom another way.

First, we'll see what Cuddlepie did. Well, he hadn't gone very far when a tram came along and stopped near him. There were a lot of people sitting in it.

"That looks an easy way of getting about," thought Cuddlepie. So he jumped on.

A tram came along

Presently a tram conductor came round.

"Tickets!" he said.

"No ticks on me," said Cuddlepie.

"I said 'tickets'," said the conductor.

"You mean little ticks?" asked Cuddlepie.

"I mean Tickets," shouted the conductor.

In Big Bad City

At the Artists' Studio

(see page 88)

Poor Cuddlepie

"I don't know them," said Cuddlepie.

"'Ere, none of your cheek," said the conductor. "Out you get, quick sticks!"

Poor Cuddlepie got off, and the tram rattled away, leaving him in the middle of the road.

The street was full of people hurrying about.

A man carrying a bundle of bush pencils (burnt sticks) went past, and as he went by some pencils dropped. Cuddlepie picked them up. The man had gone; a bright idea came to Cuddlepie.

"I'll draw some pictures on the ground, and the people will give me money," he said to himself.

He found a flat rock and drew his pictures; but, though lots of people passed, no one gave him any money, and no one noticed his little pictures.

All day long he sat there.

Once, when he wasn't looking, someone stole his clothes, which he had taken off because it was so hot; but now the sun was sinking and it grew chilly, and poor little Cuddlepie felt tired and hungry and cold.

He was lost

"I'll go back now," said Cuddlepie to himself. "Perhaps the others have got some money."

But when he looked to see which way he had come, he couldn't remember. He hurried about, first one way and then another; but it grew darker, and poor little Cuddlepie ran along the street calling, "Snugglepot! Where are you? Winky Jerboa! Ragged Blossom! Oh! Oh! Oh! Where are you?"

And as he ran along he cried bitterly, for he was lost.

A Strong Nut

"Odds pods! What's this?" said a voice from a doorway.

Cuddlepie stopped. A funny big Nut was looking at him.

"I don't know where I am," sobbed Cuddlepie.

"Well, well!" said the funny Nut.

"I—I'm lost," sobbed poor Cuddlepie.

"Dear, dear," said this funny man. "Poor little chap, come in and tell me all about it"—and, so saying, the kind funny man carried shivering little Cuddlepie into his warm house, and wrapped him in a big rug, and gave him some warm milk.

And as he is quite safe and comfortable, we'll leave him for a while and see what happened to Snugglepot and Ragged Blossom.

Snugglepot didn't walk very far before he came to a gate with a notice on it—

DOCTOR HOKUS STICKUS

Wanted, a strong Nut to mix strong medicines

"I'm strong," said Snugglepot, and in he went.

Dr Hokus Stickus looked him up and down, and all round, and in his mouth, and counted his fingers and toes, and said—

"Know how to chew gum?"—"Yes."

"Suck sap?"—"Yes."

"Squeeze juices?"—"Yes," said Snugglepot.

Dr Hokus Stickus

The Little Creek

"Gather slug slime?"—"Yes," answered Snugglepot.

"Split hairs?"—"Yes."

"Mix ant odour?"—"Yes."

"Catch cockroaches?"—"Yes, Sir."

"Bite-o," said the Doctor. "You'll do; come in and start."

So Snugglepot found work almost at once, you see.

Bush Babies

Now, what about Ragged Blossom?

When she left Snugglepot and Cuddlepie she wandered into a paddock. There was a noisy little creek running through it, and it gurgled and sang so merrily that Ragged Blossom felt quite happy.

"I'll just go with it," she said; "it's sure to lead to a nice kind of work."

So on she trotted, and as she went she found beautiful flowers—little tiny ones by her feet and tall ones high above her head. Then she heard voices, and, looking about, she saw numbers of Bush Babies coming towards her—Boronia Babies, and Wattle Babies, and Flannel Flower Babies, and lots more.

"Are you the new model?" they all cried.

Ragged Blossom felt very shy and couldn't say a word.

"Come along," they shouted. "They're all waiting for you", and, without stopping for Ragged Blossom to reply, they caught her hands and ran her along with them over the moss to a beautiful house. They opened a door and pulled her in. "Here she is," they cried joyfully.

Ragged Blossom looked up and saw a long, wide room full of queer people, all sitting and standing about as if they were waiting for something.

A little artist man came hurrying forward. He smiled at her gently and said, "You're late, but never mind, you'll make a very nice model."

Then he put Ragged Blossom up on a high place, and all the funny people began to draw her. She had to stand very still.

"Shall I get some money," asked Ragged Blossom, "if I stand quite still?"

"Of course," answered the little man, and all the time he kept walking about and telling the other funny people how badly they were drawing.

Poor little Ragged Blossom wasn't used to being a model, so she soon grew very tired, and fell in a heap and lay there fast asleep. The artist man, thinking she was ill, ran out to call his wife; and they carried her upstairs and put her into a beautiful soft bed, all hung with spider-web curtains.

"Poor little petal," said the artist's wife, "she must be very ill. Run, dear, and get the Doctor."

"I will, dear," said the artist, and, dashing out, he ran and ran and didn't stop till he reached the house of the great Doctor Hokus Stickus.

"Bless me, of course I'll come at once," said the Doctor, when he had heard the story. "And you," he said, turning to Snugglepot, "come with me. Bring the sapping dish, and the cutter, in case we may have a chance to chop off something." And so saying, he gathered up some rolls of leaves and some extra strong medicine, and they all hastened to the artist's house.

When they reached the bedside, imagine the surprise and joy with which Snugglepot looked upon little Ragged Blossom lying there in the big bed.

"It is my little friend," he exclaimed.

"Ragged Blossom," he called, "look at me. I am Snugglepot. See, I am here."

"Come," said the Doctor, "let us go away, she is only sleeping."

So they all crept out of the room.

Snugglepot leant across and gently shook Ragged Blossom.

"Wake up! Wake up! Little Blossom," he called to her; but Ragged Blossom still slept. And while Snugglepot was looking at her, wondering what he should do, he heard a great noise outside— shouts and yells. He ran to the door and looked out, and there, just coming up over the top of the stairs, was the great wicked Captain, the bad Banksia man.

Snugglepot banged the door and fastened it, and leant against it with all his strength; but he felt it opening.

"Ragged Blossom," he screamed, "come and help me! Help! Help!" he shouted.

Little Blossom sat up and blinked her eyes, then she scrambled out of bed.

"Come and help, Blossom," called Snugglepot; but, even as he

Snugglepot Holds the Door

Caught

called, the door burst open, and in rushed the bad Banksia man. With one great hand he grabbed up poor little Blossom, who was putting on her dress, and with the other he clutched Snugglepot from the ground where he had fallen.

It was all done in the winking of an eyelid. Down the stairs, out of the house into the dark, and away and away sped the bad Banksia man through the Bush, cracking the branches and crushing the flowers as he ran.

Down into the Clear Green Sea

Down, Down, Down

WHEN the Banksia man ran out of the artist's house with Snugglepot and Ragged Blossom, he put them into a big bag and threw them from a high cliff, right into the sea.

They fell out

"Ha! Ha!" roared the wicked Banksia man. "Now they'll be drowned. Ha! Ha!"

As he said this, a great Sea Eagle who was passing heard the words and saw the bag fall.

"I wonder what's in that bag?" said he, and he swooped down and caught it in his strong claws; but, as he had hold of the bottom of the bag, Snugglepot and Ragged Blossom fell out and went down, down, down, right into the clear green sea. But they weren't drowned at all; they were not even hurt. They went gently to the bottom, upside down, and two old Fish Wives, who were gossiping, screamed with fright and swam away.

"Oh! I can't stand," said Ragged Blossom, kicking about and struggling to get to her feet.

"What a funny voice you have," said Snugglepot, who had managed to turn himself the right way up by holding to a bush of seaweed. "It sounds like a brook, and just look at the bubbles!"

Ragged Blossom laughed, and up went more bubbles.

The Hermit Crab

"Now I'm up. Oh dear!" she added as she turned upside down again.

"Hold on to me," said Snugglepot. "That's right," and they both clung to the sea bush and laughed and laughed.

"Do you feel wet?" asked Snugglepot.

"I'm wet all over," said Ragged Blossom, "but I don't feel wet."

"Neither do I," said Snugglepot. Then they laughed and laughed till they forgot to hold on to the bush and over they went, upside down again.

This made them laugh more; and they laughed so much that it was quite a long time before they could stand up.

When they did they were astonished to see two big creatures struggling and fighting quite near them.

"Oh!" said Snugglepot, "they'll kill each other. They're very fierce—let's hide in here."

With great difficulty, and much turning upside down, they managed to reach the doorway of a little house, and from there peeped out and watched the battle. At last one chap was beaten and scrambled off. Then to their horror they saw the other one come crawling over straight for their hiding-place.

They shrank back, as two long sticking-out eyes came peering in the doorway.

"Great claws!" exclaimed the big creature. "Who are you? What are you doing in my house?"

"Nothing," said Ragged Blossom, trembling with fright.

"Who are you?" asked Snugglepot boldly.

"I'm a Hermit," he answered, "and this is my new house. If you are looking for a house you may have my old one."

"Thank you," said Ragged Blossom.

"Is there anything wrong with the old one?" asked Snugglepot, as politely as he could.

The Moving House

"Too small," said the Hermit, "but it would fit you."

"Thank you," said Snugglepot.

"You may have this one later on," said the Hermit, getting into his house tail first.

Away they went

"Is that one too small?" asked Ragged Blossom.

"No, but it soon will be," said the Hermit. "You see I keep growing, and every time I grow I need a larger house."

"Oh!" said the two Nuts.

"Now," said the Hermit, "I must be off. Are you ready, Anemone?" he added, addressing a creature that was sitting on the roof.

Ann Chovy Pleads with John Dory

"Who's that?" they asked.

"A friend of mine," said the Hermit, standing up and preparing to go. "You may come with me too if you like," he said. "Get on the roof and I'll take you along."

"Thank you, Mr Hermit," they both said with delight.

They clambered upon the house and away they went.

It was hard work holding on while the Hermit scrambled down the steep hillside. Just as he was climbing down, over a very large rock, he missed his hold and they went rolling down, down, right over the tops of a lot of houses and into the middle of a street.

A crowd of Fish Folk came swimming round them—such strange people—all pressing close to look at them. The Hermit had gone and, there being nothing to hold on to, Snugglepot and Ragged Blossom were bobbing about on their heads again.

"What's going on here?" asked a loud, fierce voice.

"It's John Dory," murmured the crowd, and they all stood back, for John Dory was a very important Fish Folk.

"Who are they? Where do they come from? What are they standing on their heads for?" he shouted.

Everyone was afraid to speak as he strode along and picked up Snugglepot and Ragged Blossom and stood glaring around at the crowd.

"Do they belong to anyone?" he roared.

Everybody seemed too nervous to say anything. But little Ann Chovy, who was very brave and gentle, went forward and said, "Oh, please don't hurt them. Give them to me, I like them."

John Dory was so surprised at anyone speaking to him so boldly that he fell in love with Ann Chovy then and there. "If you will promise to marry me," he said, "I'll give them to you."

Now Ann did not love John Dory, but to save the lives of poor Snugglepot and Ragged Blossom she said, "Yes, I will marry you."

When he heard her answer, savage John Dory became quite

Ann Chovy's Garden

gentle and gave her the Nuts to keep, saying, "They are yours; if anyone hurts them, he shall dry." For in Fish Land "dry" means the same as "die". Fish Folk cannot stay long out of water, just as Humans cannot stay long under water.

So Ragged Blossom and Snugglepot went to live with Ann Chovy. They were very happy. Ann made them new caps of green seaweed, with trimmings of tiny pearls, and she gave them a lovely little fish called Frilly. He was a dear little fish—pure black and white, and so clever. He followed them everywhere, and they soon grew to love him.

Ann Chovy's house stood in the middle of a lovely garden, with flowers and trees of every colour growing in it. Snugglepot and Ragged Blossom were delighted, and sometimes helped the old gardener—who had lots to do, for sea flowers don't grow in

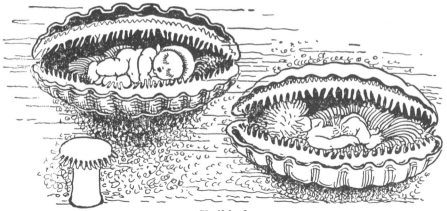

Shell beds

the ground like land flowers. They are alive and move about; so every day the gardener had to put the plants back in their places, and every night, when no one was looking, they walked away again.

At night Snugglepot and Ragged Blossom went to bed in funny little shells jutting out from the wall, and every morning they awoke to the sound of the fishes bubbling in the garden. Fish Folk call singing bubbling. For breakfast they ate sea grapes, and for tea they had prawns. The prawns were so small they didn't know they were being eaten, so it didn't matter.

At first Snugglepot and Ragged Blossom didn't enjoy eating so much wet food; but after a few days they got quite used to it, and they both thought it splendid never having to wash.

"Doesn't anybody ever wash down here, Ann Chovy?" asked Snugglepot.

"No," answered Ann, "but of course we have to scrape."

"What's 'scrape'?" asked Ragged Blossom.

"Scrape the weeds and barnacles off," explained Ann.

They went to see the sea horses in their stables, and played with Ann Chovy's beautiful red and yellow dogs. Little coloured fishes swam about overhead. "Just like birds do in the Bush," said Ragged Blossom.

"Oh, let's go down the road and see what we'll find," said Snugglepot.

"Oh, yes," said Ragged Blossom, "but where is Frilly?"

"He's helping Ann Chovy get flowers for the Dance tonight," said Snugglepot.

As they walked along the dogs came bounding after them. The road went winding through a big forest of sea-trees, and bright, wonderful flowers grew among the coral. Presently the dogs grew very excited; they had found a catfish up a sponge-tree.

"It's like a Possum," said Snugglepot. "Come here, Poss, Poss, Poss."

The catfish, thinking he said, "Puss, Puss", came down and rubbed itself against his legs.

"Oh, isn't it a beauty!" said Ragged Blossom, stroking its fins. "Let's take it home to Ann." But the catfish swam away.

"Oh, what a pity!" cried Ragged Blossom. "Let's follow it."

The Dogs had a Cat up a Sponge

Dry, or be Eaten

As they hastened along, the ground became quite clear, and a little way off they saw a funny little house at the foot of a tall sea fan. At the door sat a very, very old Fish Folk. The catfish swam to him, and he seemed very glad to see it, calling it by a strange name.

The old man was covered with shells and weed, and when he saw Snugglepot and Ragged Blossom he came hobbling towards them. "Little live Humans," said the old man in a watery voice. "Ah me! Ah me! They'll dry, or be eaten."

"What do you mean?" asked Snugglepot.

"Dry or be eaten," repeated the old man.

"Why?" asked Snugglepot.

"Dry or be eaten," said the old man, shaking his head.

"Who will eat us?" asked Snugglepot.

"Savage John Dory, greedy John Dory," said the old man.

"But he promised—" began Snugglepot.

"Ah me! Ah me!" said the old man. "Savage John Dory, greedy John Dory."

"But what shall we do?" asked Snugglepot.

"Find little Obelia," answered the old man.

"What did you say?" asked Snugglepot.

A Lovely Present

But the old man seemed not to hear, and stood shaking his head and muttering, "Little Obelia, Obelia, Obelia. Poor little Humans, dry or be eaten."

Snugglepot and Ragged Blossom looked at each other.

"I'm so frightened," said Ragged Blossom.

"Never mind," said Snugglepot, "Ann won't let us be hurt."

Mr and Mrs Bottlenose Schnapper and others

"Dry or be eaten," said the old man.

"Come," said Snugglepot. "Let's run home and tell Frilly."

But just then the old man lifted up his hands in horror and turned and ran into his little house, followed by the big cat.

Looking up, they saw John Dory and Ann riding towards them on their large dragons, leading two lovely little dragons.

The Little Dragons

"Oh!" said Ann. "You naughty little Nuts, I thought you were lost. See the beautiful present John has brought you."

Ragged Blossom and Snugglepot were so delighted that they quite forgot their fears. They jumped upon the little dragons, and they all rode home together.

Slender Long Tom and Mrs Butterfish

The dogs had gone back to Ann and told her how dangerously far the Nuts had strayed.

"Now," said Ann, while they were dismounting, "we must all hurry in and undress for the dance. Fish Folks are very like Humans in some ways."

Important Fish Folk

The dance was a very grand affair. All the important Fish Folk were there—Mr and Mrs Bottlenose Schnapper and their daughters—Mr Leather Jacket—Mr and Mrs Flathead—The Hon. Mrs Rock Whiting—Mr Pigfish and Mr Spotted Pigfish, his cousin—the Groper family—stout little Mrs Butterfish—the Red Mullets—the Breams —Lord Giant Boarfish—the Salmons —Mr Jewfish—several of the Kingfish family—Mrs Murray Cod—Mrs Beardie—numbers of the Mullet family— slender Long Tom, with his aristocratic relations, the Lardy Garfish and exclusive Mrs Sergeant Baker—Ann's cousin, Miss Oxeye Herring—the Rev. Sardine—and many others.

Rev. Sardine

Ragged Blossom and Snugglepot sat on their little stools and watched the dancing. The great hall was lit with balls of phosphorescent light, which flashed on the dancers as they floated about. There was a wonderful band of trumpeters and drummers. Most of the dresses had beautiful finish, which means trimmed beautifully with fins. Brilliant little fishes swam about among the dancers, making a gorgeous decoration.

"Come and see the supper," said Frilly, swimming through the dancers to them.

"Where have you been?" asked Ragged Blossom.

"Ann told me to keep guard in the supper room," said Frilly,

The Wonderful Ball

"and to see that the decorations don't get out of place. It's kept me busy."

"Oh dear!" said Ragged Blossom, "don't you wish you had flowers like our Bush ones? They don't walk about."

"I do," answered Frilly.

When they went into the supper room, Frilly darted forward. "Goodness!" he exclaimed. "Just look at those cucumbers."

Three of the prettiest cucumbers had climbed off the table and were hastening to the door.

Three sea cucumbers

"That centre vase has moved," said Frilly, fussing about and rearranging the table. "Sit still," he cried, smacking the beautiful plant with his fin. Carefully swimming all about the table, he pushed everything into place with his nose.

"Oh! Frilly," said Snugglepot, suddenly remembering, "we saw a funny old man this afternoon, and he said John Dory was savage and greedy.

Just as Snugglepot said these words they heard a movement among the sea lilies. Turning, they saw the glittering eyes of big John Dory looking fiercely at them. His mouth was too full of food to speak, but he looked so angry that Ragged Blossom wanted to run away. Frilly whispered to them, "Stay still."

"If you please, Sir," said Frilly to John Dory, "Miss Ann would like to know if you are satisfied with the supper table."

"Tell Miss Ann," said John Dory, "that it would look better if the two Nuts were seated on a dish in the centre." And with a terrible smile, and working his big jaws up and down, John Dory strode out of the room.

Frilly turned very pale. "Little friends," he said, "you must go at once—come quickly—with me." So saying, he led them, as fast as they could go, out at the back of the house, down to the stable. There they found to their dismay that every horse and dragon had gone.

"What shall we do?" whispered Snugglepot.

"I don't know, I can't think," said Frilly.

"Oh, if we only had the little Obelia! The old man said we must find Obelia," said Ragged Blossom.

"What!" exclaimed Frilly. "Tell me quickly, what about Obelia?"

Snugglepot hastily told him.

"Why," said Frilly, "I know, I can find her. Oh! quickly, quickly, come with me."

Swiftly and with care Frilly led them to a little shell house on the big wall of the garden. There he stayed with them through the long night. When the early morning light was creeping in, they left their hiding-place.

"Now," said Frilly, "I'll take you to school. You will be quite safe there. Besides, John Dory will be sleeping all day after his supper—he always eats and eats and eats till he can scarcely move."

"Poor Ann," said Ragged Blossom. "She's going to marry him to save us, and now he's going to eat us after all." Ragged Blossom began to cry.

"Don't cry," said Frilly. "If I can find little Obelia, no one

At School with the Little Fish Folk

can harm you, and I think I know. Oh, be quick! Go into school and say nothing, but just sit among the children and learn lessons. I will call for you by and by; now I must hurry, for I've much to do."

Ragged Blossom and Snugglepot sat very still in school and learnt of the many dangers that beset the lives of the Fish Folk.

In the lunch hour they played games with the little fishes, who were all very nice to them, though they stared at their noses, for some of the Fish Folk haven't any noses at all.

When they went into school again Snugglepot had a bright idea. "Please, teacher," he said, putting up his hand, "do you know about little Obelia?"

The teacher, who was very kind, though mournful, looked at Snugglepot sadly.

"Ah," she said, "poor little Nut. Your education has been neglected. Every child here knows the story of Obelia. Goggle-eye," she said, addressing one of the big girls, "stand up and tell these poor children the story of Obelia."

"Yes, miss," said Goggle-eye; and this is the story she told:

"Once there was a beautiful woman sailing in a great, enormous ship on the top of the sea, and she was the slave of a great and wicked King. She was so unhappy that she threw herself into the waves, and as she sank her soul went out and became a beautiful pearl which lay among the weeds at the bottom of the sea for a thousand years. It is written in the Great Scales of the Fish Folk Book that, when live Land Folk come near it, the pearl will open like a white flower and within will be found a tiny little baby, whose name shall be Obelia. No harm shall come to those who love Obelia, and she shall grow up to be the Princess of the Fish Folk."

"Thank you, Goggle-eye, you may sit down," said the teacher.

The Shadowy Form

"I wish I could find it," said Ragged Blossom.

"But has anyone seen it?" asked Snugglepot.

"Of course not," answered the teacher. "Attention, please; we'll take the next lesson."

When school was over, Frilly was waiting outside to take Snugglepot and Ragged Blossom home, and on the way he told them of the plans he had made.

"Now," said he, "stay close to Ann all the evening till it's bed-time; then, when everyone is asleep, creep out of the back door and come to the garden gate. I shall be there."

"Very well, Frilly," they both said. "We'll do everything you say. Oh, isn't it exciting!" and they ran away to find Ann.

That night, when all was still, Snugglepot and Ragged Blossom stole softly down from their shells and out of the house.

"What is that dark thing there?" whispered Ragged Blossom, shrinking back. Something was moving among the anemones, so they crouched down in the shadow and watched.

"It's John Dory," whispered Snugglepot. "He's looking in at our bedroom window. Come away quickly."

So saying, Snugglepot took Ragged Blossom by the hand, and they ran and ran till they reached the garden gate.

Looking behind, Snugglepot saw the shadowy form of John Dory stealing after them behind the trees.

"What is the matter?" said Frilly, as they rushed into his fins.

"John Dory!" gasped Snugglepot.

"Quick, then," cried Frilly, "jump up", and he helped them onto the horses he was holding.

"Now," he said, darting out, "follow me", and away they went.

Looking back, Snugglepot saw two glittering eyes peering round the gate after them.

Most Wonderful Things

When they had galloped through the town and out into the Forest, Frilly came up to them. "Let the horses rest now," he said. "The tide is running this way and will carry us along."

So they rested and went easily, floating along.

"Are we going far, Frilly?" asked Snugglepot.

"Very far," answered Frilly.

What a wonderful journey it was!

Though it was night-time, all the way was lit with phosphorescence. They were riding along among the weeds on a steep hillside, and down in the deep below they could see huge fish swimming past and strange shapes floating about.

"Isn't it gummy!" said Ragged Blossom, keeping close to Snugglepot.

"Tree top," answered Snugglepot.

"What's that big noise up there?" asked Ragged Blossom.

"That's the blowing of the Whales," answered Frilly. "They go up to the top to breathe."

"Oh, look!" cried Snugglepot, "look at all those great snakes right away down there."

"That's an Octopus," said Frilly.

"I'm frightened," cried Ragged Blossom.

"Don't be afraid," said Frilly. "I can scent them a long way off, and I know how to dodge them."

"Oh, what are those lovely things floating over there?" asked Ragged Blossom.

"Those are Sea Comets," said Frilly.

And so they went on and on, seeing most wonderful things all the way, Frilly guiding them carefully all the time and keeping them from danger.

At last the dark began to fade away, and a soft green light stole about them.

What They Found

"Now," said Frilly, "you must leave the horses, for we have to do some climbing."

Tying the horses to a sea fan, they followed Frilly up a steep coral wall. Above their heads were beautiful curtains of seaweed, and in and out among them swam little golden fish, all striped with brilliant colours.

"Go very gently," said Frilly, as they neared the top of the wall. He was very excited and fluttered his fins and tail nervously.

Ragged Blossom and Frilly were the first to reach the top. Frilly darted over. Ragged Blossom gave a cry of joy.

There, almost touching her, floated a wonderful pearly white flower, and resting asleep in the middle of its petals was a tiny pale baby. Its little hands and feet were pink, and on its little round head were fins of gold and green. It glowed in the pale green light of the morning, and Ragged Blossom and Snugglepot and Frilly made no sound, so filled with wonder were they.

As they all looked, the little baby stirred, opened its blue eyes wide and, looking straight at Ragged Blossom, held out its tiny arms.

"Frilly, Frilly," cried Ragged Blossom. "Look, it wants to come to me."

In her excitement Ragged Blossom leant too far over and tumbled head first into the deep hole over which the little baby was floating.

Frilly darted forward to catch her, but she fell so fast that he could not reach her. As she sank, he swam after her, trying to catch her frock in his mouth; but as they went deeper it grew darker, and presently it was so dark that Frilly couldn't see at all.

"Where are you?" he called, but no answer came, and as he swam about in the dark a strange thickness seemed to gather in the water and nearly choked him.

The Finding of Little Obelia

Giant Squid

With great difficulty he swam up again and reached the place where he had left Snugglepot. He was gone! Frilly rested on the wall, panting, and looked about him.

The beautiful white flower had closed its petals, and all the little golden fish were swimming round and round it faster and faster, so that, as the black water rose from the hole, the little fish kept it from touching the white flower.

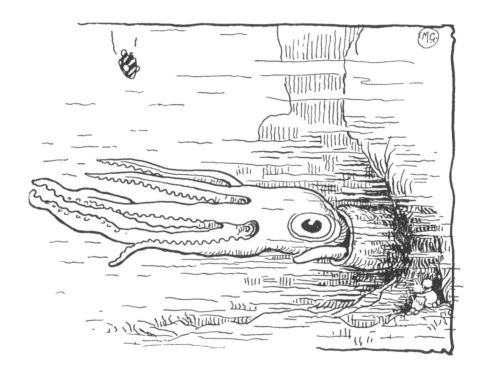

"Something very terrible must be going on down there," thought Frilly, and, being very brave, he dived straight down again into the black water. Down and down he swam, till at last he came to the bottom. The water cleared a little, and he could just see a great Giant Squid sitting glaring at him from the door of his cavern.

The Terrible Giants

Frilly started with horror, for there in the dark of the cavern he saw the pale faces of Snugglepot and Ragged Blossom.

"What do you want?" growled the Giant, waving his long arms about. Frilly was so afraid that he couldn't move or speak.

The Giant stretched out a great arm towards him, but, just as he was about to catch hold of Frilly, a huge creature dashed past and, with great jaws wide open, struck the Giant a mighty blow.

Quick as lightning Frilly darted into the cavern, and, seizing Ragged Blossom by the dress, he put his head under Snugglepot, lifting him on to his back, and swam out of the cavern. The two Giants were struggling and groaning, and the water bubbled and foamed about them.

"Hold to me," said Frilly, as he panted and swam along.

Slowly they went, further and further away from the terrible Giants, until at last they reached the top of the wall. Poor Frilly sank upon the coral as if he were dead. Snugglepot and Ragged Blossom bent over him in distress.

"Oh! Frilly, dear Frilly," said Blossom, "how brave you were! Poor Frilly, we were so heavy, and you have saved us."

But Frilly soon recovered, and then they remembered the little baby. Looking round, they saw to their delight that it was still there, and the lovely white petals were opening again and the little fish were pushing it towards them.

At last it was so near that Ragged Blossom leant forward and, taking the baby gently out, clasped it safely in her arms. Thereupon all the little bright fish seemed to go mad with joy, for they leapt and plunged and swam about Ragged Blossom in a wonderful way, singing—

> "Obelia! Obelia! Obelia!
> Love will she give,
> Long may she live,
> Obelia! Obelia! Obelia!"

Riding Home on Dragons

(see page 104)

Homeward

So they took the little baby and, mounting their horses, began the homeward journey.

Now we shall leave them and see what Cuddlepie has been doing all this time.

They began the homeward journey

A Big Surprise

WHEN the kind Nut carried Cuddlepie into his house, who do you think was sitting in his easy chair, comfortably reading a book and smoking his pipe?

Why! dear old Mr Lizard, as large as life.

So utterly astonished was Mr Lizard that he sprang high up out of his chair, and knocked a hole in the ceiling.

Cuddlepie ran to him with a shout of joy and hugged him.

Kind Mr Nut looked on in great surprise. "I'd better get somethin' ter eat an' drink," he said, and hurried out of the room.

Then Cuddlepie and Mr Lizard had a long talk, and, when Cuddlepie had told his story, Mr Lizard looked very solemn indeed.

"And where are Snugglepot and Ragged Blossom now?" he asked.

"I don't know," said Cuddlepie, "I've lost them."

Mr Nut's Goodies

"Then," said Mr Lizard, springing up again and making another hole in the ceiling, "I must be off at once, this minute. Great Snakes! My Bully Ant! Oh, Gum!" And with that he dashed out of the door and was gone.

At this moment Mr Nut came in, carrying a tray of good things to eat.

"Stop!" he shouted to Mr Lizard. "Wait! I've some lovely cakes", and in his anxiety to stop Mr Lizard he jumped on his disappearing tail—whish went the tail, and over went Mr Nut, and down went the tray full of goodies.

"Putt! Putt!" said Mr Nut, getting up and rubbing himself. "What a pity! Such nice ones. All dirty. I'll have to cook all day tomorrow now."

"Could I help you?" asked Cuddlepie.

"Yes, yes," said the kind Nut. "Good idea! Now we'll go to bed, and don't you worry, little chap. In the morning Mr Lizard will come back with news of your friends. He's a mighty clever chap, is Old Man Lizard."

So they went to bed, and Cuddlepie was so tired that he slept soundly till the sun was high in the blue and all the city was up and dressed long since.

Cuddlepie found Mr Nut in the kitchen hard at work making cakes.

"I'm sorry I'm late," said Cuddlepie. "Please let me help."

"Dear, dear, of course," said Mr Nut, and he gave Cuddlepie some pollen and dew to mix.

It was such fun making cakes that Cuddlepie forgot all his troubles and was quite happy.

Cuddlepie Learns to Cook

A Grand Invitation

Now Nuts do all their cooking with the heat of the sun, so they have to cook enough cakes and things to last over the days when there isn't any sun.

Mr Nut was a baker. Cuddlepie was so useful all the morning that Mr Nut said he could live with him and drive his cart round if he liked.

Cuddlepie was delighted; and Mrs Prying Mantis, who was peeping in at the sun-hole, went away and told all the neighbours that Mr Nut had a new baker man, and how nice-looking he was, and all the clever things he could do.

The news went round till it came to the big, soft ears of Mrs Bear. Now, Mrs Bear was big and fat and rich, and she was one of those people who liked doing things other people didn't do, so that all her neighbours would say "How clever!" and "How strange!"

So she thought, "I'll give a big party and ask this Baker Boy to come and do all his tricks, and it will be the talk of the place."

Next day a large invitation card came.

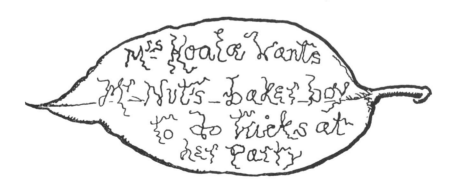

"Odds Pods!" exclaimed Mr Nut. "That's a grand invitation. You must go, of course. Dear, dear! Putt! Putt!"

Mrs Bear's Party

A Wonderful Idea

Now Cuddlepie didn't know any tricks at all; but he wanted to go to the party, so he thought and thought all day and all night. He lay awake thinking how he could do some clever trick at the party, and as he lay there the Frogs were singing and croaking out in the night, and while he listened to them a wonderful idea came to him.

He jumped out of bed and went down to the swamps and had a long talk with the Frogs. Then he went home to bed again, and as he fell asleep a happy smile settled on his face.

On the morning of the party a large cart drove up to the door of Mrs Bear's house.

"Mr Cuddlepie, the Baker Boy, sends his best wishes, and will Mrs Bear allow his pianola to be put into her parlour, so that he can play to her tonight?" said the Serve Ant.

Mrs Bear was most delighted, and the workmen struggled in with a great tree trunk, so large that it took ten Workers and twenty-five Serve Ants to carry it.

Fortunately Mrs Bear's house was very very large, or the pianola wouldn't have gone through the doorway.

News went round the neighbourhood that something wonderful was going to happen at Mrs Bear's party. So all the people who were asked dressed early and went off in great excitement; and so great was the crowd that a lot of people who were not invited slipped in without being noticed.

When Cuddlepie arrived, very late, everybody pressed close to look at him, and all the important visitors shook hands with him.

Then Mrs Bear said, "Will you play us something on your wonderful pianola, Mr Cuddlepie?"

And Cuddlepie, looking very grand and grown up, bowed and said, "That's what I'd like to do, Mrs Bear."

What Cuddlepie Heard

Then he sat on a stool by the tree trunk, and put his feet upon the bark pedals, and worked them up and down as hard as he could, and there came forth a most wonderful noise. For the tree trunk was hollow, and there were a hundred frogs hidden in it, and the largest one had his eye to a hole to see when it was time to begin and when to stop.

The harder Cuddlepie worked the pedals, the louder the frogs sang. When Cuddlepie stopped they stopped, because Mr Frog at the peep-hole gave the signal.

Everyone was amazed, delighted; they had never heard such a beautiful noise.

"So loud!" said Mrs Kookaburra.

"So like a creek!" said Mrs Bear.

"Just like moonbeams!" said another.

"So beautiful to talk to!" said Mrs Parrot. Every time Cuddlepie played his pianola, Mrs Parrot talked louder and louder.

"You know, my dear," she was saying to Mr Owl, "when my friend, Mr Eagle, saw the Banksia man throw the bag into the sea, he swooped down and caught it; but, as he did so, out fell a Blossom and a Nut. Wasn't it——"

"What?" screamed Cuddlepie, who had heard all she said.

The music died away, and everyone gasped as Cuddlepie sprang upon Mrs Parrot and seized her wing.

"Tell me! Tell me!" he cried, "what did Mr Eagle see? Were they drowned? Oh, oh, tell me!"

"I don't know, I—I really don't know," stammered Mrs Parrot.

"I can tell you," said Mr Possum. "I know the story. They fell into the mouth of a big fish and were swallowed."

Goodness Me!

"That's all wrong," chuckled Mrs Kookaburra. "Quite wrong. I had the story from Mr Shag, who was an eyewitness. He saw them sink, and dived in after them. They went straight to the bottom and were drowned."

At these words Cuddlepie became very pale, and cried, "Who will go with me and show me where they fell into the sea?"

When Cuddlepie said this, everyone jumped up, and everybody wanted to go; but nobody knew where to go, and everyone talked at once, and all the frogs hopped out of the pianola; but no one noticed them.

"Come with me," said a voice close to Cuddlepie's ear, "I can help you", and, turning, he saw Mrs Kookaburra.

"Are they friends of yours?" she asked, as they hastened out of the house.

"Yes," said Cuddlepie, his tears falling. "My brother Snugglepot, and my friend Ragged Blossom."

"Goodness me!" said Mrs Kookaburra. "How dreadful! Now, if you'll ride on my back, I'll take you to see my friend Mr Shag. He knows Mr Eagle, and between them we shall surely learn something."

Cuddlepie climbed onto Mrs Kookaburra's broad back, and away she flew. They very soon reached the sea, and Mrs Kookaburra flew slowly along the coast looking for her friend.

"He may be anywhere," she explained. "He loves travelling."

Once they passed a seaside place where lots of Nuts and Blossoms were surfing. They all looked so happy, and poor Cuddlepie felt so miserable that his tears kept dropping as they went, and the people looked up to see if it was raining.

At the Seaside

Home to Ann

For many days they flew up and down the coast, till at last one day they heard a shout; and looking down they saw, far away below them, standing on the branch of a dead tree waving to them—who do you think? Why, old Mr Shag himself.

So Mrs Kookaburra flew down, and great was their joy at finding him at last. They all made a little camp for themselves, and while they are sitting there talking we'll go back to Snugglepot and Ragged Blossom.

You remember we left them riding home with the dear little baby. Snugglepot and Ragged Blossom each carried it in turn, and Frilly was the proudest fish that ever wagged a tail.

"How did you know where to find her, Frilly?" asked Snugglepot.

"That's a secret," said Frilly. "Do not ask me, I dare not tell you."

"But what was that terrible Giant doing there?" asked Ragged Blossom.

"Hush!" said Frilly. "I may not tell you any of these things."

"Oh," said Ragged Blossom, holding Obelia closer to her. "Perhaps he is a Wicked Spirit and has held her all these years."

"Perhaps," said Frilly, "and maybe he is dead now. The Sperm Whale is a strong Giant."

When at last they reached home they found Ann Chovy in tears and great distress.

"Oh, my dear Nuts," she said, "I thought you were lost."

Then Ragged Blossom held up the baby.

The Flying Fish Races

Great Rejoicings

At the sight of it Ann lifted up her hands in joy and amazement, and soon Trumpeters were sent forth to spread the news, and great was the joy of the Fish Folk.

Now it chanced that John Dory was away upon a journey, so the children were relieved, and a great merrymaking went on in the

Playing Trammel Net

Fish Folk Town. Flags were hung out, and bands played, and everyone was glad. All the Fish Folk children had holidays, and the Sea Urchins went wild.

Ragged Blossom and Snugglepot joined in the sports, playing

trammel net, and riding races upon Flying Fish, a sport much loved by the Fish Folk.

Each day they went driving in Ann's carriage. Ragged Blossom always carried Obelia, for everyone must know that she belonged to Ragged Blossom.

After many days of happiness a shadow fell upon the town—John Dory returned.

He looked pale and tired, and went about angry and silent. Like magic the merrymaking ceased. Everyone spoke in whispers and wondered what would happen next.

One day Ann came to Ragged Blossom greatly distressed.

"Dear little Blossom," she said, "you and Snuggle-pot must leave me. Go at once, or I fear some great harm may befall you."

As she said this, Ann wept and clasped her hands in sorrow.

"Oh! Ann," said Ragged Blossom, weeping too, "where shall we go?"

"Anywhere, anywhere, only go quickly and hide, and send Frilly secretly to tell me how you are from time to time."

"But, oh, what about baby Obelia?" said Ragged Blossom.

"I will care for her," said Ann.

"Oh, I could not leave her," answered Ragged Blossom.

Out Riding with Ann Chovy

Fresh Adventures

So it came about that Ragged Blossom and Snugglepot rode out from Fish Folk Town, and left their dear Ann, taking with them little Obelia and the faithful Frilly.

When they had travelled a far way they rested in a small village. There they made for themselves a little home. The Fish Folk round about were kind to them, and they lived contentedly, Snugglepot and Frilly hunting for food while Ragged Blossom kept house and cared for Obelia.

After a while luck came to them. On one of his rambles Frilly found a large hook baited with beautiful meat. It hung in a clean sandy spot, and always in the same place.

"Let's open a butcher's shop," said Snugglepot, when Frilly told him of his find.

"Splendid!" said Frilly. "We shall make a lot of money."

So they moved their little house to the spot and built a shop.

It was splendid. As fast as they cut off the meat, the hook was hauled up and reloaded and let down again, always in the same spot.

They made lots of money from the rich Fish Folk, but when any poor Soles and old Fish Wives came they gave them meat for nothing. But alas, one day the hook went up and didn't come down again.

"What shall we do now?" they all said in dismay.

"I know," said Ragged Blossom. "We'll start a laundry. Baby needs so many things, and we can wash them all at the same time."

Snugglepot and Frilly agreed, so they moved house again and started business.

One day, while Ragged Blossom was scraping a large coat, she turned the pockets and out fell a note. It was large writing, and, to her great surprise, she saw her own name on it.

The Butcher's Shop

The Laundry

Two Letters

Picking it up, she read it all. This is what it said:

Dear Octopus,

One million pearls, all of Coral Point, and half the Bay of Clams shall be yours if you find me the baby Obelia and the two Nuts called Ragged Blossom and Snugglepot.

Your faithful Fish Folk,

JOHN DORY

When Ragged Blossom read this her little heart nearly stopped beating.

Who was Octopus? What should they do?

Hardly had she time to think before she saw Snugglepot and Frilly hastening towards her.

"Great news," called Snugglepot, waving something. What do you think it was? A gum leaf!

"Look!" said Snugglepot, breathlessly. "We found it—the hook was hanging in its old place, and on it was this letter. Hear what it says: 'I am up here; cling to the hook, and I will pull you up. Your friend, Cuddlepie.'"

"Oh," said Ragged Blossom in amazement, "Oh, Cuddlepie, dear, dear Cuddlepie! I am glad."

Then she remembered the letter she had found. "But see," she exclaimed. "Look what I found in that coat."

"Great Starfish!" exclaimed Frilly. "Old Octopus! He's a friend of the Giant Squid. He lives in the Bay of Clams. He is terribly fierce."

"I'll Bite Your Head Off!"

"We must go at once," said Snugglepot.

"There's not a moment to lose," said Frilly, and even as he spoke they heard a great commotion in the village.

"It's John Dory," exclaimed Frilly. "Oh, hurry," he cried.

Snugglepot caught Ragged Blossom's hand and they ran half swimming to the door. It was too late—there stood the terrible John Dory; but the doorway was small and he stuck half-way.

"Quick!" gasped Frilly, pushing Snugglepot and Ragged Blossom back. "The other door"—but there was someone there. "The window," shouted Frilly, and he lifted up Ragged Blossom and tumbled her through. Then he pushed Snugglepot up, but just as he was getting him through, John Dory rushed round the house and caught him. Frilly darted out of the door behind John Dory, and fastening his teeth into the back of his neck he bit and bit furiously.

"Where is Ragged Blossom?" growled John Dory, shaking Snugglepot fiercely.

"I won't tell," said Snugglepot, kicking with all his might, while Frilly kept on biting, and John Dory could not reach him to knock him off.

"Find me Ragged Blossom, or I'll bite your head off," shouted John Dory.

"I won't," said Snugglepot, kicking again.

"Stop!"

"Then here it goes!" said John Dory, choking with rage, and with that he opened his huge jaws and put Snugglepot's head right into his mouth.

"Stop!" screamed a voice so sharply that John Dory looked round to see where it came from.

He put Snugglepot's head right into his mouth

John's Love for Ann

It was Ann. Her great dragons came galloping almost on top of them. Ann sprang from the carriage, rushed to John Dory, and pulled Snugglepot from him; then she fell fainting to the ground with Snugglepot clasped in her arms.

John Dory, who, though he was so greedy and so cruel, really loved Ann, was quite grieved to see her lying there so white, and he said gently, "Ann, dear little Ann, look up." But Ann lay quite still, and her eyes were shut, and her arms hung limp beside her.

Then John Dory felt real distress. "Oh, speak to me, Ann," he said, his big hard face growing gentle while his hands trembled with fear. "Oh, Ann, tell me, where are you hurt?"

Then Ann's big eyes slowly opened and looked at him.

"Here I am hurt, John," she said, putting her hand to her heart.

"But what—what hurts you there?" asked John.

"You, John," said Ann, looking at him, "you are so greedy, so cruel, so fierce, that you terrify me—I dry", and her eyes closed again, her head fell back and she lay as dead.

At these signs John fell upon his knees beside her, clasped her hands, imploring her, "Come back, Ann, stay with me; I will never be fierce again, never greedy, never cruel. Never shall I terrify you; gentle and kind I will be to you, Ann, and to all creatures in the sea. I swear by the fins of Neptune."

Now, when Ann heard these words, she opened her eyes and seeing the truth in John's face, that he meant what he said, she put her arms about his neck and smiled upon him.

And as all the Fish Folk in the sea can tell you, from that day to this John Dory was a changed creature—though, it must be written, he is the only one of his family that has ever been known to be so.

Quite Safe

Snugglepot and Frilly had remained struck with wonder by all they saw, and, when Ann rose and asked where Ragged Blossom was, they seemed to wake from a dream.

But Ragged Blossom, who had been hiding near by, came running to Ann and threw her arms about her.

There lay the tiny baby

"Oh, Ann," she sobbed, "we have to leave you for ever and we are going back to the Bush; our dear friend Cuddlepie has sent a message."

Then John turned away to hide his gladness, for he could not bear that Ann should love these Nuts.

"But where is little Obelia?" asked Ann.

"She is sleeping," answered Ragged Blossom as she lifted the lid of a shell, and there lay the tiny baby, fast asleep.

"Then I shall keep her for you," said Ann, "and love her and care for her just as you would have."

"But," exclaimed Ragged Blossom, "I shall take her with me."

"Up to the land," cried Ann and Frilly together. "She will dry," they said with horror.

"Dry?" gasped Ragged Blossom.

"Most surely," said Ann.

"Oh yes, surely," said Frilly.

"Oh, Snugglepot," cried Ragged Blossom, "let us stay here."

"I can't," said Snugglepot, "I must go to Cuddlepie. He is my brother. I must go."

"Oh me! Oh me!" cried Ragged Blossom. "I will come, but let us go quickly or my heart will break."

So they all went to the place where the great hook was.

There it hung, throwing a great shadow over the clean sand.

In silence they kissed Ann and shook hands with John, and hugged Frilly, and kissed the baby sleeping in Ann's arms. Then they both put up their hands to take hold of the great hook. Ragged Blossom looked back at little Obelia, and as she did so, little Obelia opened her eyes and, looking at Ragged Blossom, held out her arms to her.

"Oh," cried Ragged Blossom, jumping down, "I cannot go, I cannot go." And, running to the baby, she caught it from Ann and held it fast.

Good-bye

"Good-bye, dear Snugglepot," she sobbed. "Good-bye, good-bye."

Then the big hook began to move up slowly. It lifted higher and higher, far up over their heads, and Snugglepot rose with it, growing smaller and smaller, till at last he faded out of sight.

Out Into the Sunshine

IT was a long way to the top of the sea, but·Snugglepot clung to the hook, and, when at last he came swinging out into the sunshine, it so dazzled his eyes that he couldn't see. The air was so light after the water that he felt quite giddy; and what with sorrow at leaving Ragged Blossom and joy of going back to Cuddlepie, poor Snugglepot felt strange and weak, and would have fallen back into the sea if two big, strong hands had not caught him.

"Is that you, Cuddlepie?" called Snugglepot, for he still couldn't see.

"Ha! Ha! Ha!" laughed a great rough voice. "So you thought it was Cuddlepie, did you?

On a post sat a shag

"Ha! Ha! That's a good joke, that is. Ha! Ha! Ha!"

Snugglepot shivered. He knew that voice—it was the Captain—the bad Banksia.

"Cuddlepie," called Snugglepot. "Cuddlepie help! help! help! Cuddlepie!"

He shouted with all his might and someone heard him. A long way off on a post sat a shag who had been posted there by Mr Shag. He knew the name, and at the first faint sound of it he sent it along to the shag on the next post, who passed it on again; and so it travelled from post to post.

"Cuddlepie," they screamed. Each shag took up the cry, and it passed along from post to post, quicker than I can tell you. That is why we talk of sending things by post.

The News

In a very short time—only a snap of the fingers—before the bad Banksia had stopped laughing, Mr Shag had the news. He told Mrs Kookaburra, she flew off to tell Mr Eagle; Mr Eagle found Mr Lizard; and Mr Lizard told Cuddlepie.

Such was the excitement and eagerness among the friends, that at first they all rushed about, getting in each other's way and doing nothing.

But Mr Lizard soon found his head. "Mr Eagle," he said, "you carry Cuddlepie to the spot and keep your eye open for the enemy on land. Mrs Kookaburra, you get a bed ready in case anyone's hurt. Mr Shag, you go along the shore and give us the signal from the sea."

And with that Mr Lizard dashed away through the bush.

Cuddlepie jumped upon Mr Eagle's back, his bag of stones across his shoulders, his sling in hand. Straight and swift flew Mr Eagle, high into the sky. Mr Shag went low over the water, and Mrs Kookaburra skimmed the tree tops. Everyone kept an eye on Mr Shag.

Presently he rose, then dropped like a stone into the water. It was the signal. Down swooped Mr Eagle, a huge stone clutched in his wonderful claws.

As they came down they looked below, and here they saw a terrible thing. All the bad Banksia men were sitting in their boats, laughing and clapping their hands, and looking up at a high cliff. There, on top of the cliff, stood the baddest of all the bad Banksia men. In one hand he held poor little Snugglepot, and in the other a great stone. At his feet was a deep, deep hole.

"Here he goes. This is the end of him!"

"Now," he shouted to the other Banksia men, "here he goes. This is the end of him." Then he held Snugglepot over the hole, and was just going to drop him in when, with a terrible shout, out sprang Mr Lizard, right upon the bad Banksia man. Snugglepot fell from his grasp and rolled away, right to the edge of the cliff; but a dear little plant that was growing there stiffened and held him from falling, even though it suffered in doing so, for plants are kind to the Nuts.

Then began a great struggle. First Mr Lizard was uppermost; then the wicked Banksia was on top. Sometimes they rolled about; sometimes they rose upon their feet again, and all the time they drew nearer and nearer to the edge of the cliff.

Mr Eagle swooped down. Plump, he let the great stone fall, and down went one boatload of Banksia men. Then Cuddlepie took aim with his sling, and bizz! a sharp stone caught the bad Banksia man in the back; but he only held poor Mr Lizard the tighter. Mr Lizard was fast losing his breath.

"In another moment he'll be over," shouted Cuddlepie, as Mr Eagle rose with another big stone.

Plump went the stone, and down went another boat full of Banksias. Bizz! went a stone from Cuddlepie's sling, and this time it hit the bad Banksia man on the head. Over he went, his fingers loosened from Mr Lizard's throat; and just as both were toppling into the sea Mr Eagle swooped down and caught Mr Lizard.

Splash! went the Banksia man, down, down, into the sea, and never a Banksia man was left to tell the tale.

"Snugglepot! Snugglepot!" called Cuddlepie, jumping from Mr Eagle and running to his side; but Snugglepot lay still.

The Terrible Fight

Deadibones

Very gently they carried him to the bed prepared by Mrs Kookaburra, and then they all sat round—Mr Lizard panting still and bruised, Mr Shag all dripping with sea, Mr Eagle and Mrs Kookaburra—all watching to see if his eyes would open—and they did!

"Cuddlepie," he cried, springing up.

"Snugglepot," cried Cuddlepie, hugging him tightly.

"Where's the Banksia man?" asked Snugglepot.

"Deadibones," said Cuddlepie.

"Good root," said Snugglepot, and he fell asleep again, and slept and slept, for he was worn out. When at last he woke and told them how Ragged Blossom had stayed behind to take care of little Obelia, Cuddlepie wept sorely, for he missed his little friend.

"Don't cry," said Snugglepot, "she will be quite happy with the Fish Folk and dear Ann and Frilly, and by and by we may be able to go down and see them all."

So Cuddlepie cheered up and they said good-bye to Mr Shag, and Mrs Kookaburra, and Mr Eagle.

Mr Lizard, being rested, made a bed and slung it upon his back; and in that way he carried Snugglepot beside Cuddlepie all the long, long journey, away, away back to their old home—and

Everybody Happy

great was the rejoicing when the dear mother and father once more clasped their little Nuts to their hearts.

And this is the end of the Second Book of the Tales of Snuggle-pot and Cuddlepie.

Little Obelia

and more about Snugglepot and Cuddlepie

Little Obelia

LITTLE OBELIA, AND FURTHER ADVENTURES OF
RAGGED BLOSSOM, SNUGGLEPOT AND CUDDLEPIE

HERE begins the story of Little Obelia.

Now tell me: Do you really think all the bad Banksia men were deadibones when they went to the bottom of the sea in the great fight with Mr Lizard and Mr Eagle and Cuddlepie?

Were they deadibones?

Not a bit of it! Not one of them!

When they came to the bottom of the sea, they sat up and rubbed the places where the stones had hit them, and gazed about.

As they sat there peering through the seaweed, a large carriage

drawn by sea dragons floated above them and passed quickly out of sight.

"Did you see that?" gasped the biggest bad Banksia man. "It was Ragged Blossom."

"What?" shouted all the other bad Banksia men.

"It was Ragged Blossom, I tell you," he cried. "Squeeze and breeze her!"

"Root and shoot her!" growled one.

"Stone and bone her!" spluttered another.

"What's the good of talking?" said the biggest bad Banksia man. "We must follow and catch her; this is the way they went. Come on!"

Then one of the bad Banksia men said it wasn't the way, and they all began fighting and quarrelling about it. So great was the commotion that numbers of fish came swimming round.

The bad Banksia men stopped quarrelling and stared with wonder at the strange creatures. Suddenly a huge fish came at them with its mouth wide open, and was about to swallow them; but they turned and were just in time to save themselves by running into a curious house hidden amongst the tall sea flowers. Just as the last bad Banksia man was squeezing in, they shut the door too soon and left his leg sticking out; the big fish darted at it and bit it off, and then went nosing round looking for more.

Inside the house the bad Banksia men huddled together and shook with fear.

"Ha! Ha!" croaked a terrible voice.

A Threat

Clutching each other, the Banksia men stared into the dark corner where the voice seemed to be, and there they saw a dreadful eye looking at them. As they gazed in terror, out stole a long, creeping, crawling arm, and seizing one of the Banksia men drew him slowly into the dark corner. The big eye glared at them all the while.

The bad Banksia men were so terribly afraid that they couldn't move or speak.

Then the horrible voice croaked again. "All of you, one by one. I shall eat all of you."

And as the Banksia men stared into the dark corner, they saw a great bulgy monster with lots of long, creeping, crawling arms, and what do you think it was doing? It was eating up the bad Banksia man!

Now when they saw this terrible sight, all the other Banksia men fell on their faces and called aloud, "O monster, spare us. We will be your slaves. We will find for you the beautiful Ragged Blossom, that you may eat her. Only spare us." And they wept, and tore their hair, and rolled about in their fear.

But the great monster silently went on eating up the Banksia man, till not one little bit was left.

"Now," said the monster, "where is this Ragged Blossom? Can you fetch her to me?"

"Yes, yes!" cried the Banksia men, looking up.

"It is not enough," said the monster, "I want more."

"We will bring you Nuts from the Bush above."

"How many?" asked the monster.

"Two," said they.

"I must have hundreds," said the monster.

The Bargain

"We will bring them," cried the Banksia men.

"Very well!" said the monster. "You shall be my slaves and bring me plenty of Nuts to eat, and if you fail me I shall eat you all, all, all."

So the bad Banksia men became the slaves of the wicked and awful Giant Octopus.

Mr Lizard at Home

I TOLD you how Mr Lizard carried Snugglepot and Cuddlepie on his back all the long, long way home, and how happy their mother and father were to see them again. You remember that?

Well, just imagine how excited all the Blossoms and Nuts were when they heard of the wonderful city of Big Bad, and how Snugglepot had lived under the sea with the Fish Folk; and, most exciting of all, how poor little Ragged Blossom had stayed behind at the bottom of the sea, because she could not bear to leave the little baby Obelia.

Very well then!

One warm spring day Mr Lizard sat smoking in his cool sitting-room, thinking how blue the sky was through the window and how sweet the wattle scent was coming in through the door, when he heard a step on the verandah, and in walked Snugglepot.

"Stump and bump me!" exclaimed old Mr Lizard, jumping up and shaking him by both hands.

"By Gum! I am glad to see you. Slip your cap and sit down and tell me all the news."

"I've been thinking about Ragged Blossom," said Snugglepot.

"And so have I," cried Mr Lizard.

"And so has Cuddlepie," continued Snugglepot.

"Well, well!" mused Mr Lizard, "that's strange."

But stranger still—at that very moment, while they were talking of her, little Ragged Blossom, far, far away at the bottom of the deep green sea, was sitting before her phosphorescent fire, fast asleep, dreaming that she was back in the Bush again with all her dear old friends. Now, wasn't that strange?

Ragged Blossom Dreams

Mr Lizard Asks Questions

"Yes, we've been thinking," continued Snugglepot, "that if she stays down in the sea too long she'll turn into a Fish Folk and never be able to come out again."

"Can't the Fish Folk come out then?" asked Mr Lizard.

"Goodness, no! they'd dry," said Snugglepot.

"Go deadibones?" asked Mr Lizard.

"Quite," replied Snugglepot.

"Dear, dear!" murmured Mr Lizard. "What a dreadful thought! Now, what's to be done?"

"We think of going down to fetch her up," said Snugglepot.

"I'll come too," Mr Lizard roared excitedly, smacking his tail. "I'll most certainly come."

"Good root!" cried Snugglepot.

"And now that's settled," said Mr Lizard, "let's go along and see the cricket, eh?"

Snugglepot agreed, and off they went.

"I suppose you'll be very glad to go down and see your friends the Fish Folk?" asked Mr Lizard, as they strolled along.

"Oh, yes!" answered Snugglepot, "I love Ann Chovy."

"John Dory's a bit of a queer fish, isn't he?" asked Mr Lizard, picking a spray of native rose to flip the flies off with.

"He used to be, but he's quite changed now," said Snugglepot.

"And this baby Obelia: found in a sort of pearly thingumbob, wasn't it?" asked Mr Lizard.

160

"We found her," said Snugglepot proudly, "so we kept her. That's why Ragged Blossom stayed behind when I came up."

"Dear, dear!" said Mr Lizard, who had often heard the story but enjoyed hearing it all over again. "And she's a sort of lost what-you-may-call-it?"

"Princess," said Snugglepot. "And she's to be Queen of the Fish Folk when she grows big."

"Well, well, now!" said Mr Lizard, stopping and hunting for his spectacles and, when he found them at last, putting them on and looking solemnly at Snugglepot over the top. "A Queen, eh? Well! well! And you think little What's-her-name——?"

"Obelia," put in Snugglepot.

"Will be old enough to be left by now?"

"Quite," said Snugglepot.

"Hum!" Mr Lizard took off his spectacles, and they strolled on again. "Well, well! So that's it, is it? Dear me! By the way," he suddenly remembered, "where's Cuddlepie?"

"Gone to the dentist," Snugglepot told him.

"Ah," said Mr Lizard, "that's a place I never go to. There ought to be a law against them. Well, here we are."

Having arrived at the Cricket Ground, they found a little grassy bank and sat themselves on it, quite unconscious of a long dark form that had followed them all the way, and two bright black beady eyes that were watching them from a bush near by. It was a most exciting match, and they forgot all about everything in their enjoyment of the game.

At last it was over, and they turned homewards. As it was still very warm, Snugglepot suggested that Mr Lizard should drop in with him and have a cool drink, and discuss plans for the journey. Mr Lizard agreed, and in they went.

"What will you have?" asked Snugglepot, going to his useful little cupboard. "Juice of sour suds, aphis milk, or some old sap?"

"Three drips of old sap and fill it up with dew, thank you."

So they quenched their thirst and drew their chairs together and lit their pipes.

There was a window in the room they were sitting in, and before it hung a beautiful cobweb curtain. So earnestly were they talking that they did not notice a dark shadow, which had been on the curtain, slowly move across and disappear.

"So the plans are safe?" sighed Mr Lizard.

"Safe as the river bank," Snugglepot assured him.

Suddenly there was a loud knocking on the door.

"Come in," called Snugglepot.

No one came in.

"Who's there?" cried Snugglepot, going to the door and opening it.

There was nobody there.

"That's airy," exclaimed Snugglepot, "nobody there."

"Nobody?" Mr Lizard was puzzled, so he went and looked out.

"Not a whiff," said Snugglepot.

The Cricket Match

Under the Bed

Now, while they were gazing out of the door, something slipped silently in through the window, crossed over the floor and glided under Snugglepot's bed.

"Ah, well," said Mr Lizard, going back to his chair, "some silly soot playing jokes, I suppose. Now, let's get to earth and settle our affairs."

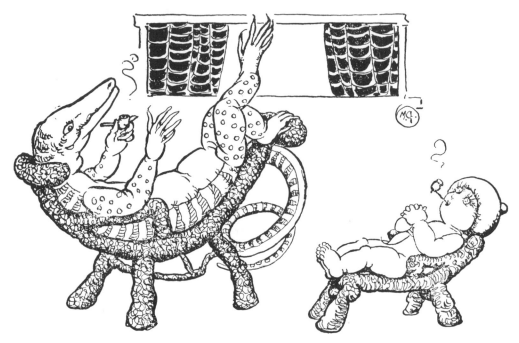

They pulled their chairs closer together, and talked long and earnestly in low whispers; but not too low for every word to be heard by the two ears sticking out from under the bed close behind them.

At last Mr Lizard got up.

"Well, I must be going," he said, knocking out his pipe. "Don't forget, tomorrow at birdrise by Little Creek waterfall. I'll go round and let the rest of the Nuts know. Take care of the plans. Grig, grig!"

Knock on the Door

"I will," said Snugglepot, "and——"

Another loud knock on the door startled them. They both rushed for the door, tumbling over each other in their hurry.

"Hullo!" shouted Snugglepot, flinging open the door, "who's there?"

It was growing dark.

"Nobody again," said Snugglepot, peering out.

"Extraordinary!" cried Mr Lizard, peering out also.

Neither of them saw a shadowy form that crept silently out from under the bed, glided to the window and, climbing noislessly through, disappeared into the dark.

Going to the Dentist's

As Cuddlepie walked along towards the dentist's, he began to feel more and more miserable.

"I hate dentists," he said aloud. "I'd sooner be deadibones than go there. Suppose I don't go!" He sat down on a log to think about it.

As he sat there, resting his sore face on his hand, a Blossom came running along the road, sobbing bitterly.

"Why, what's the matter?" asked Cuddlepie kindly.

"Too-too-too-too-toothache!" sobbed the little Blossom.

"Oh come with me," said Cuddlepie cheerfully, "and I'll show you a nice kind dentist. He'll soon cure you."

And taking her hand he led her gently down the road.

They had not gone very far when they came upon Mrs Bear sitting by the roadside, rocking to and fro and groaning deeply.

"What's the matter, Mrs Bear?" asked Cuddlepie and the little Blossom.

"Oh, oh, oh," groaned Mrs Bear, "I've got a dreadful face-ache."

"Then come along with us, we're going to the dentist. He'll cure you, he is so kind."

Mrs Bear stopped groaning, got up heavily from her seat, and lumbered along behind them.

Not very far on they came to a little hut; there was a terrible noise inside—shrieks and yells—so they all stopped. Cuddlepie ran up and banged on the door.

"What's up?" he shouted. The growls and yelps stopped.

Mrs Bear and the Rest Follow

Mr Possum opened the door.

"I'm trying to uproot a tooth, and it won't let go," he moaned.

Cuddlepie persuaded him to join the party, telling him how nice and kind the dentist was, and off they set again.

Presently they came to a little grey furry kangaroo, who was hitting his head with a stick as hard as he could.

"Oh, don't," they all cried, "you'll hurt yourself."

"That's just what I want to do," answered the kangaroo, hitting himself harder than ever.

"Goodness," said Cuddlepie, "why do you want to hurt yourself?"

"I like it better than toothache," the kangaroo moaned.

"Dear me!" said everybody, shaking their heads at each other, "another one."

"You'd better follow me to the dentist," advised Cuddlepie.

"He's so nice!" said Blossom.

"So kind!" murmured Mrs Bear.

"So gentle!" put in Mr Possum. "A dear!" they all cried.

"Wait a jump," said the Kangaroo, "I'll fill my pouch and hop after you quicksticks."

A dismal howling greeted them at the next corner, and running over to a fence they found Mrs Dingo and six little yellow dingoes, with their heads up, yowling piteously. The little dingoes told them their mother had toothache.

At the Dentist's

The Poisonous Person

"Never mind," said Cuddlepie, "come and see the dentist, Mrs Dingo, and the little Dingoes can see the teeth pulled out." So they joined the party and trotted along after the others.

They all hopped, flumbered, and trotted along after Cuddlepie, gathering more Bush folk as they went, till quite a crowd was following him.

At last they reached the dentist. They found the waiting-room so crowded that most of them had to stay outside.

"Gummy!" said Cuddlepie with a sigh of relief. "No good me waiting!" and off he went, so happy at getting away from the dentist that he sang and jumped about as he went along.

"It's funny," he said aloud, "what a long, long way it is to the dentist, and what a little way it is coming back."

"I've noticed that too," said a voice in his ear.

Cuddlepie was startled and looked about, but could see no one.

"It seems strange," said Cuddlepie to himself, "that everyone should have toothache today."

"Quite simple," answered the voice, "there's a sale on at the honey shop."

"Where's that voice?" cried Cuddlepie, stopping and looking round everywhere.

"Here it is," chuckled the voice mockingly, and out from a hole right at his feet popped the head of Mrs Snake—not Mrs Snake that was killed outside the Gum Inn, of course, but another Mrs Snake—Mrs Black-Snake. Cuddlepie jumped back. He knew what a poisonous person Mrs Black-Snake was.

"It's a warm day," murmured Cuddlepie politely, moving off and trying to look unafraid.

Deceitful Mrs Snake

"Middling hot," said Mrs Snake, "but don't be in such a hurry; I've news for you."

"News?" cried Cuddlepie.

"From a friend of yours who lives in the sea."

Cuddlepie stood still, astonished.

"Who do you mean?" he stammered.

"A letter from little Ragged Blossom to you," answered Mrs Snake, coming right out of her hole and swaying about near Cuddlepie till he felt his back go all creepy.

"If you come with me," she said softly, curving herself a little closer, "I'll show you. I found it floating in the creek; it was sticking in the wing of a shag that was——"

"What?" asked Cuddlepie eagerly.

"Deadibones," chuckled Mrs Snake.

"How?" asked Cuddlepie, shocked.

"Humans, I suppose. Good thing too, I hate shags," she added venomously.

"I s'pect you hate everything," said Cuddlepie.

"Why should I?" hissed Mrs Snake.

" 'Cause everything hates you," and Cuddlepie looked hard into her wicked little eyes.

"That means you do," wheezed Mrs Snake, flicking her forked tongue in and out and stretching out her neck till she was only a few inches from Cuddlepie's face.

"S-s-s-so it's yes, is it?" she hissed, getting nearer and nearer and swaying her head backwards and forwards.

A Strange Sleep

"S-s-sle-eep! S-s-sle-eep! S-s-sle-eep!" she hissed, and Cuddlepie still looked into her eyes. Now they seemed to grow bigger and bigger, and nearer and nearer, and then they faded away, for Cuddlepie had fallen into a sleep, a strange sleep.

Mrs Snake had hypnotized him, just as she does poor little birds and other Bush creatures.

"Now," she said, "perhaps you'll have the goodness to follow me." And Cuddlepie did.

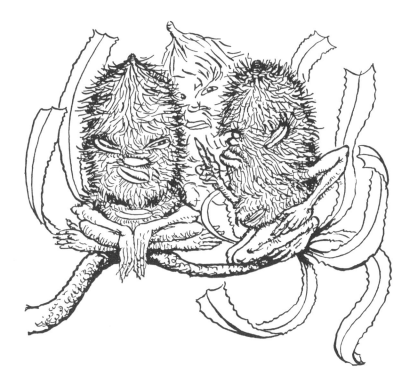

Not very far away a number of Banksia men were sitting in a Banksia-tree, basking in the sun and planning mischief.

Looking down, one of them spied Mrs Snake and Cuddlepie.

"Ah!" he cried, jumping about and shaking the bough till all the Banksia men's heads were knocking together, "there's one of 'em. She's got him!"

"Bunch and scrunch 'im!" shouted one.

"Hit and spit 'im!" growled another.

"String and ring 'im!" snarled a third.

Then they all jumped about, grunting and chattering and shaking the bough till the leaves rattled.

"S-s-s-stop that noise and listen to me," commanded Mrs Snake, twisting her body into a knot of annoyance. "I've had a letter from the big Boss Banksia man."

All the Banksia men touched their toes with their heads to show their respect for the Boss Banksia man.

"He is down in the sea, and the rest are with him. The Giant Octopus has them in his power. We are to catch and send him the slimy sinners Snugglepot and Cuddlepie, and as many more Nuts as we can trap, for only so can they escape being eaten by the Giant."

"And what do we get for our trouble?" growled a little stubby Banksia with red hair and squinny eyes.

"More than you deserve," hissed Mrs Snake. "The Boss is sending wonderful treasure; it is to be laid in the cave by the sea at Big Bad City."

"Where's Mr Snake?" asked the red-haired Banksia man. "Why can't he do something?"

"He's spying on 'em now," snapped Mrs Snake. "About time you made some plans yourselves 'stead of leaving it all to me."

"It's your pleasure," snarled a big black Banksia man; "you enjoy it."

"So do you," said Mrs Snake, spitting her tongue in and out

at him. "Come on," she added, turning to Cuddlepie. Twisting and wriggling her body in anger, she slid away into her hole.

Mrs Snake's house consisted of one big room at the end of a long passage. It was a cool room with a round window in the ceiling. The window was open, and over it hung trails of delicate green maiden-hair fern.

Pulling Cuddlepie in after her, Mrs Snake tied his hands and feet with strong grass, pushed him into a corner, and rolled a heavy stone against him.

"There!" she said. "Now I'll go out and find something to eat; there's not a morsel in the house." And smiling a wicked sly smile she slid out and away up the passage.

You remember Winky Jerboa, the poor little stowaway, and how unhappy he was when he went home to Big Bad City and found that all his people had gone away? Well, he kept the house and garden tidy, laid in stores, and waited; but neither his mother nor father nor sisters nor brothers ever came back, so poor little Winky left home again and roamed from place to place, hoping that some day he might find them. So here we see him limping with tiredness, carrying his bundle like any old tramp.

"This looks a nice cool place," he said, dropping his bundle and sitting down beside it. "I think I'll rest."

Help!

The afternoon was warm, and the scent of the rock-lilies made him drowsy. Slowly the long lashes closed over his big brown eyes, and lower and lower drooped his weary head, till at length he sank right down upon the cool green moss, sound asleep.

A tiny brown lizard ran over him, but Winky did not stir. A big blue butterfly lit upon his little damp nose; his whiskers twitched, but Winky did not wake.

A spider, letting himself down from the fern above, landed upon the tip of his soft ear, but Winky did not wake.

Two kookaburras flew into the tree overhead and laughed and chattered for quite a while, but Winky did not wake.

Some big frogs croaked in a pool near by, but Winky did not wake.

A bright green beetle climbed clumsily all the way along his tail, but Winky did not wake.

Two Willy Wagtails came and danced about all over him, but still Winky did not wake.

Mrs Snake came out of her hole, saw Winky, and exclaimed, "Such a sight! Food at my very door."

Then Winky awoke. He sprang up as if he had been blown up, and as he sat up he shrieked "Help!"

Now a cousin of Mr Lizard's happened to be driving down the road, and on hearing the cry he pulled up his bandicoots.

"Help!" came the cry again, but it sounded fainter this time.

Mr Lizard sprang from his wagon and rushed into the bush. There sat poor little Winky, white and stiff with fear. Reared before him, ready to strike was the terrible Mrs Snake. Though Mr Lizard was only a little chap, he sprang upon her without a moment's hesitation. In a flash he had her by the neck, his strong hands squeezing her till she squealed for mercy.

The Escape

"Run!" called he to little Winky, "run for your life and don't stop till you're home."

Poor little Winky was so frightened that at first he could hardly move.

"Run! Run!" shouted Mr Lizard, for he felt her slipping.

So while they fought and rolled about, Winky picked up his bundle and dashed away as fast as his tired little legs could carry him.

He ran and ran, till suddenly the ground gave way beneath him, and he fell—crash—thud—right into the middle of—where do you think! Why, right into Mrs Snake's house. But he wasn't hurt, so he picked himself up, and was about to dash out of the door, when he noticed something lying in the corner.

"Cuddlepie!" he gasped in amazement. "Poor Cuddlepie; some-one has done him deadibones. Oh, poor Cuddlepie", and he untied the bands and lifted him up.

At this moment there was a rustling noise, and there in the doorway swayed Mrs Snake. Winky was frozen with horror.

"Ah!" hissed Mrs Snake, raising her head, "I have you." But as she spoke her throat swelled, her eyes turned purple, and with one bound into the air she fell at Winky's feet; and there she lay, for she was wounded.

Winky saw his chance; holding Cuddlepie tightly in his arms, he sprang clear across her body and out of the door. Staggering and stumbling, he found his way up the dark passage, and at last, with a cry of relief, fell out into the sunshine. But there was no time to lose.

Half carrying and half dragging poor Cuddlepie, he managed

to find a hiding-place in a hollow tree. Oh, joy! A door opened, and there stood kind **Mr Possum**.

Pleese not without entering

"Take us in . . ." panted Winky. "Mrs Snake! . . . Oh, be quick!"

Without waiting for more news, Mr Possum helped them in, and what's more, Mrs Possum took poor Cuddlepie and bathed his face and gave him medicine and soon brought him out of his strange sleep.

"What has happened?" asked Cuddlepie, opening his eyes.

They told him.

"There must be mischief about," said Cuddlepie. "I must hurry home." Then he saw Winky and there was more talk.

"Stay here till it gets quite dark, and then I'll see you on the way," said kind **Mr Possum**.

So they did.

Not at Home

THE moon was up, full and round, when Cuddlepie and Winky, having said good-bye to Mr Possum, stopped at Snugglepot's house and knocked at the door.

All was still within. Cuddlepie knocked again; no answer. They both knocked; not a stir inside.

Then they knocked and shouted, and shouted and knocked, and made so much noise that a party of Nuts, returning very late from the Gum Inn, asked what the matter was.

"We can't get in," said Cuddlepie.

"Climb through a window," suggested a Nut.

"It's too high!" answered Cuddlepie.

"Oh, that's easy," laughed the Nuts, and before you could say Robin-red-breast they had piled themselves each upon the other's shoulders till quite a long ladder was made. But it was just too short, for when Cuddlepie climbed up he could only catch the window sill with one hand.

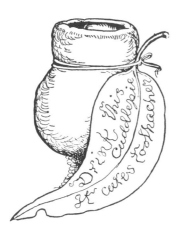

Suddenly Winky, who was looking on, ran like lightning up over all of them and clean in at the window. Once there, he easily helped Cuddlepie in. So they thanked the Nuts, who then unmade the ladder and went their way.

When Cuddlepie looked about he found to his astonishment that Snugglepot was nowhere to be seen.

"What's this?" said Winky.

In the middle of the table was a mug,

They Made a Ladder

and tied to it a leaf, on one side of which was written: "Drink this, Cuddlepie; it cures toothache", and on the other, "then come to the waterfall at Little Creek."

"How kind of Snugglepot!" said Cuddlepie. "It's just what I need. Have some, Winky?"

"No, thank you," said Winky, who didn't like the smell of it.

Cuddlepie, who was always good at taking medicine, tipped up the mug and swallowed it all. No sooner had he done so than a strange look came into his face, and he began to dance and sing and turn somersaults. Then, catching Winky by the end of his tail, he threw open the door, whisked him out, and went tearing off down the road, dragging the astonished Winky after him.

By this time it was early birdrise, and a crowd of Nuts had gathered at the Little Creek waterfall as arranged, to meet Mr Lizard and Snugglepot. When Cuddlepie and Winky bowled into their midst they all threw up their caps and laughed and sang.

Then some Nuts saw a large sign on a tree. It read:

"Who'll follow me
Down to the sea?"

and there was a newly cut track leading into the Bush.

"I will," shouted Cuddlepie, waving his cap. "Come along, Nuts", and away he went like mad, the rest all after him helter-shelter along the new track.

They had not gone far when they came to another notice saying:

"Don't turn back,
This is the track."

So on they went till by and by they came to another sign:

"This is the way,
Merry and gay."

179

Crossing the Lizard Bridge

The Long Track

Off they went again. Presently the track took a sudden downward turn into a deep gully. At the bottom splashed and gurgled a mighty stream, and here was another signboard:

"To the Lizard Bridge.
Go over the ridge."

They all turned back over the ridge, and there they saw a monster lizard standing across the stream, his front legs on one bank and his back legs on the other.

The Lizard took no notice of the Nuts or of the deep water rushing under him; he just stood there blinking sleepy eyes and licking up any stray ants that came along. All the Nuts clambered up where his tail was smallest, walked along his huge body and crossed safely to the other side—all except Cuddlepie, who, because he danced and skipped about, lost his balance when he got to the middle and fell splash into the stream.

The rushing water made so much noise that nobody heard his shout, and most of the Nuts were away up over the hill before anyone knew what had happened. When they heard about it there was much disturbance. Some were for going back; but others said, "No, it is best to go on and tell Snugglepot, who will be waiting for us."

All the Nuts agreed to this, so away they went once more, leaving little Winky Jerboa sitting in the middle of the track, weeping and wringing his hands.

At length, when the sun was high overhead, they came to another notice. It said:

"Just round the bend
Is the journey's end."

By this time they were all very tired and so hot that when they turned the bend and saw before them the beautiful wide blue sea, they threw up their caps and shouted for joy.

What Happened to Cuddlepie

Lying close beside the rocks was a fine, tall ship. They all clambered aboard, calling loudly for Snugglepot; but there wasn't a soul to be seen, and there written on the vessel's side were the words:

"If you want to find me,
Jump into the sea."

On seeing this the Nuts were delighted, and without waiting a moment they pushed the ship out from the rocks till it floated over the deep, deep water. Then, climbing onto the side, they all sprang off, just like a lot of pink frogs, and went swimming down, down, down, into the cool green sea.

Now let us leave them all and see what happened to Cuddlepie.

At first, when he found himself being carried along at such a pace, he felt afraid; but after a while he began to rather like it.

He just floated along, enjoying the scenery as it went by. It was very much like riding in a train—only, of course, he didn't know that as he'd never been in one.

Once he passed some great red kangaroos drinking at the water's edge.

Another time he was swept almost into the arms of an astonished old platypus; another time he was able to rescue a tiny baby bird which had fallen from its nest, by pushing it into a clump of green ferns as he rushed past.

Into the Cool Green Sea

Fish Folk Hospital

In almost no time at all he found himself swirling and whirling right away from the land, and out into the sea. Then something caught hold of his legs and dragged him under so quickly that he couldn't think or hear or see.

* * * * * *

When Cuddlepie opened his eyes again he didn't know where he

was. All about and above him was water, and a pale green light flooded everything. He was lying on a curious little bed sticking out high on a wall; there were numbers of other beds just like his, also sticking on the wall.

While he was looking about, a strange creature came floating up to him and gave him something queer to eat.

"Where am I, please?" asked Cuddlepie. "And what's this?"

"Fishes' eggs. You're in hospital," answered the nurse, who was a Fish Folk. Then she swam away again before he could ask any more questions.

"Scrub and rub me!" thought Cuddlepie. "How did I get here?"

Just then he heard voices. Peeping over the side of his bed, he saw to his great amazement, away down on the floor below him, walking about and talking—Well! Who was it?

The Hospital

What Ragged Blossom Saw

Why, dear little Ragged Blossom.

Cuddlepie was so excited that he swallowed all the eggs in a gulp and nearly fell out of his bed. He tried to call to her, but his head went all wuzzy and he sank back, helpless.

Yes, it was Ragged Blossom, and with her were little Obelia and Ann Chovy and a boy with a large basketful of presents for the patients. While Ann was talking to Dr Fuscus Carp and the nurse, Ragged Blossom went about comforting the patients. She liked going with Ann to cheer the poor sick Fish Folk, and she always used to pay special attention to the new patients, for she thought they would feel so lonely. So she climbed up to speak to one who looked very miserable, with his head all covered up and only a little bit of hair sticking out at the top.

"Won't you have a flower?" she asked gently.

The patient shook the bedclothes, but made no answer.

"Oh, do, please," begged Ragged Blossom.

"All right, then," snapped the patient, and popped his head out.

Ragged Blossom fell off the stool in horror. It was the great shaggy head and ugly face of a Banksia man. With a cry of fear she ran to Ann Chovy.

"Eels' fins!" exclaimed the nurse.

"Great Starfish!" bubbled the doctor.

"What's the matter, little one?" asked Ann.

"The man in the bed there," whispered Ragged Blossom. "Oh, I'm so frightened. Come home, Ann."

"He won't hurt you," smiled Dr Fuscus. "We brought him in this morning—one leg off—small boy with him—sick—like to see him?"

"Oh, come home," wailed Ragged Blossom.

Seeing that she was really upset, Ann hastily said good-bye and, taking little Obelia by the hand, hurried away.

Cuddlepie is Left Behind

Just as they were going out of the door, Cuddlepie roused from his dizziness, sat up, and saw Ragged Blossom.

"Ragged Blossom, Ragged Blossom!" he called, leaning out and waving his arms to her. "Come back! It's me—Cuddlepie. Come back! Come back!"

But Ragged Blossom didn't see or hear him; and, as the big door closed behind her, poor little Cuddlepie put his head down upon his pillow and wept.

Little Obelia

Now at last we come to little Obelia. She is very important, so listen carefully while I tell you about her.

When she was a wee speck of a baby, she lay asleep in a pearl at the bottom of the sea. All round her grew beautiful Obelia seaweeds (that is why they called her Obelia) and thousands of rainbow-coloured fish guarded her night and day. There she lay

for years and years, and while she slept a wonderful wisdom grew in her, though her little body remained the same. I can't tell you why or how, but it was so. At last, one day the pearl burst open and spread out into a beautiful white flower, and that, you remember, was when Ragged Blossom and Snugglepot found her.

From that time on Obelia grew very quickly, and now, as you see in the picture, she is as big as Ragged Blossom. And she was much wiser—so wise, indeed, that not only Ann Chovy, but John Dory and all the cleverest Fish Folk for miles round, came to ask her advice on matters of great importance.

Obelia Counts Her Pearls

So when they came home from the hospital, and Ragged Blossom told Obelia of the bad Banksia men, she went quietly to her thinking-room and counted her pearls—she always did this when she was troubled about anything. She had hundreds of pearls, some big enough to build a house with, and some so little that they were nearly out of sight.

When Obelia had counted her pearls, she went to Ann and said, "Come with me to the flower-stall man; he has something to tell you."

So they went. Ragged Blossom and Obelia hovered about, loving the beautiful flowers and putting their faces into them, for sea flowers are like land flowers—the closer you look into them, the more beautiful they seem.

Meanwhile Ann bought a lovely red bunch, and while she was paying him the old flower-seller leant close and whispered in her ear, "There is danger following you."

"How?" asked Ann eagerly.

"The little one called Ragged Blossom," whispered the old man. "The shadows are about her."

"Oh, tell me! What is it?" Ann begged.

"It is the Evil One, the great Giant Octopus. He sends his shadows out to catch her."

"Shadows?" asked Ann, trembling.

"Black shadows with shaggy heads and many eyes," answered the old man.

At this terrible news Ann grew so afraid that she called quickly to Ragged Blossom and Obelia and, thanking the old flower-man for his kindness, she took their hands and hurried home.

The Flower Stall

Then Ann told them what she had heard.

"Don't be afraid, little Gellyfish," said Obelia, kissing Ragged Blossom and clasping her tightly. "I will take care of you."

Then without another word she went to her thinking-room. Again she counted her pearls, and when she had counted the last littlest one she came back to Ann.

"Dear Ann," she said, "go back to the hospital and bring away the little pink boy."

"Oh, no!" cried Ragged Blossom. "The Banksia man is there; don't go."

"Yes, I will go," said Ann.

Ragged Blossom rushed out to the stables. She threw her arms about the neck of her favourite dragon and whispered, "Bring Ann safely back from the hospital. Go quickly and come swiftly."

Then she went to the old coachman and begged him to take care of Ann. Then she found John Dory and pleaded with him to go to the hospital also. Although he was very busy polishing his scales, John patted her kindly and said he would go.

Long and anxiously little Obelia and Ragged Blossom waited at the garden gates, and at last they saw the carriage coming in the distance. The lovely dragons came swimloping home, and

Sea Dragons in their Stables

there between John and Ann, smiling and chatting, sat little Cuddlepie.

It was a wonderful surprise. Ragged Blossom and Cuddlepie were so happy, and everyone was so glad because they were so happy, that all thought of the Banksia men and their evil shadows vanished away.

So Cuddlepie came to live with John Dory and his kind wife Ann, and learnt to play trammel net, and ride the dragons, and eat sea cucumbers. And most of all, he learnt to love Ragged Blossom's little pet fish, Frilly.

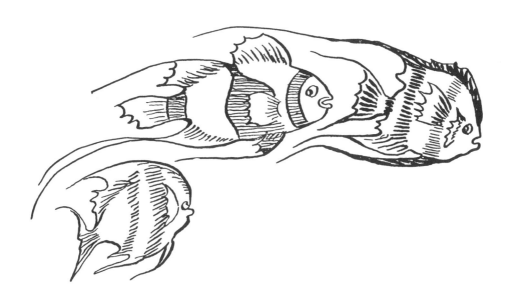

Cuddlepie Caught

BUT where do you suppose Snugglepot and Mr Lizard were all this time?

When we last saw Snugglepot he had gone to bed, and he fell asleep wondering why Cuddlepie was so long at the dentist's—you remember?

Well, he had hardly been asleep two ticks when he woke with a start. There was a loud knocking at the door. Snugglepot sprang out of bed, shouting as he threw open the door, "I'll catch you this time!"

To his great surprise there stood Mr Lizard; he seemed very upset and out of breath.

"What's the matter?" cried Snugglepot.

"Oh, Gum!" gasped Mr Lizard, sinking into a chair and fanning himself with the tip of his tail.

"Whatever is the matter?" repeated Snugglepot.

"It's Cuddlepie," moaned Mr Lizard. "He's caught."

"Caught?" gasped Snugglepot.

"The Banksia men have got him," groaned Mr Lizard. "Oh, Gum! Gum! Gum! What shall we do?"

"How? When? Who?" asked Snugglepot very excitedly.

"An old tramp came to my house and told me. He said he saw the Banksia men hit Cuddlepie on the head, put him in a bag, and run off down the road to Big Bad City lickety-plick."

Snugglepot was pulling on his travelling leaves. "We must get off after them quicksticks," he cried, reaching for his cap.

"Rag and scrag me!" shouted Mr Lizard, jumping up. "Oh, silly sooted cinder that I am! Why didn't I think of that?"

The Wicked Plot

"The plans!" cried Snugglepot, rushing to the little hole he kept them in. There they were safe enough. Cramming them into his cap, he jumped onto Mr Lizard's back and off they dashed, and in quarter less than no time there was nothing to be seen but a trail of dust down the moonlit road.

*   *   *   *   *   *

No sooner were their backs turned than two black figures stole from the shadow of the house and crept through the open door. They were two very bad Banksia men.

"Ha, ha!" laughed one of them grimly. "They swallowed the bait all right."

"Gobbled it up," chuckled the other. "Got that stuff?"

" 'Ere it is," growled the first, taking a big mug from his bag and placing it upon the table. He filled it from a bottle which he also took from the bag, and then tied a note round it.

On that note was written, "Drink this, Cuddlepie; it cures toothache; then come to the waterfall at Little Creek."

Now you know why it was that Cuddlepie went one way and Snugglepot and Mr Lizard another way; and you can guess who wrote all the notices, and who it was who caught Cuddlepie and pulled him under the sea. That would certainly have been the end of Cuddlepie if Dr Fuscus Carp had not driven by just as the Banksia man was dragging Cuddlepie along to the Giant Octopus.

Kind Dr Fuscus Carp, seeing the Banksia man had only one leg—for he was the one whose leg had been bitten off when they all rushed into the house of the Giant Octopus—took the Banksia man into his carriage and carried him to the hospital. "For," he said, "I can make you a new leg, and the little boy looks ill, so a few days in shell will do him good."

195

The Long Journey

After that the Banksia man had to do what he was told; so when he saw Ann taking Cuddlepie away he could only grind his teeth with rage, and he kicked so hard that his new leg came off and had to be fixed all over again.

You see what a wicked plot Mrs Snake and the Banksia men had made. Now what had become of all the Nuts who jumped into the sea? And where is little Winky Jerboa?

All in good time, you shall know.

First, let's go with Snugglepot and Mr Lizard and see what happens to them.

Old Mr Lizard galloped and galloped, sometimes stumbling into holes, sometimes jumping logs and scrambling over rocky places, and sometimes shying at the strange shadows cast by the moon.

Snugglepot clung to his back with great difficulty, and all night they hastened on till at last, just as a pale light was stealing into the sky, Mr Lizard could go no further, and they stopped by a little waterhole to drink.

An old tramp hobbled up to them as they were resting. "Mornin', mates," said he. "Making a long journey?"

"To Big Bad City," Snugglepot told him.

"I've just come from there," said the tramp.

The Road to Big Bad City

The Football Scrum

An Old Tramp

Mr Lizard asked him anxiously if he had passed anyone on the way.

"I seen some rough-lookin' blokes—very rough-lookin' they was. One of 'em was dragging a little cove along an' 'itting 'im over the 'ead with a stick; 'itting 'im cruel, 'e was."

Snugglepot and Mr Lizard had heard enough. With a bound Snugglepot was on Mr Lizard's back, and Mr Lizard was off up the road as if he were the wind.

The old tramp burst out laughing and threw off the cloak that covered his head. As he gazed after them he shook his fist and growled, "Travel on, there's someone waitin' for yer in Big Bad, but it ain't yer slimy Cuddlepie."

All the next day they pushed on, till at last they knew by the number of houses they passed, and the crowds of people, that they were nearing Big Bad City.

Once they were nearly run over by a motor-car, and the numbers of young Nuts on scooters made them quite nervous. Then they saw a big crowd of Nuts watching a football match; but on they went, poor Mr Lizard's tongue hanging out and Snugglepot stiff with holding on. Still on they went.

By and by they came to a big river; there were crowds of Nuts and Blossoms on the banks. Boats were racing, and the crowds were cheering. It was most exciting; but on they went till at last they came right into the great city of Big Bad.

All the time as they went along they kept asking people if they had seen a Banksia man with a little Nut. Nobody had seen them.

Mr Lizard was so tired by this time that, spying an old shed, he hobbled into it, fell down and went fast asleep. Snugglepot arranged some grass under Mr Lizard's head as a pillow and then stole out, for he was very hungry.

Boats Were Racing

The Art Gallery

(see page 206)

Just a little way up the street he came to a splendid tea shop; it was cheaper on the roof, so he went up.

"This is juicy," thought Snugglepot as he sat at a small round table and ordered some grass-root cakes and aphis milk.

"Isn't it a nice blue day?" he said to the plump blossom who was sitting opposite.

" 'Tis a scented afternoon," agreed the Blossom. "The cicadas are so trilly."

"Rippling!" said Snugglepot. "Did you see the regatta?"

"Not quite," murmured the Blossom. "Was it good?"

"Treetop!" said Snugglepot; "and the football match?"

"Just missed it," sighed the Blossom. "Was it exciting?"

"Simply bumping!" replied Snugglepot, sucking at his straw.

"My husband is an artist," said the Blossom with pride. "Why," she exclaimed, "you are the Nut who came to our house with—with——"

"Doctor Hokus Stickus," cried Snugglepot and the Blossom in one breath.

The Blossom turned quite pink. "Oh, dear," she gasped, "what a fright you've given me! I heard you were drowned in the sea."

"Only a little," said Snugglepot.

And they laughed and chatted, and by and by the Blossom asked Snugglepot to come home with her and see her husband.

"But what about my friend Mr Lizard?"

"Bring him too," said the Blossom.

"Thank you," said Snugglepot; but when he looked into the shed Mr Lizard was gone.

"Where can he be?" exclaimed Snugglepot.

The Roof Garden

The Gumnut Artist

"So strange!" said the Blossom. "But my house is only just across the road; we'll send a serve-ant to keep watch for him." So saying, she led the way to her home.

The artist was delighted to see Snugglepot and begged him to camp with them for a long time. So he did, and every day he

went out looking for Cuddlepie and Mr Lizard; but never could he see or hear anything of them, till at last he grew quite thin with anxiety.

One day the artist asked Snugglepot to come into his studio to see a picture he had painted for the important Exhibition soon to be opened. "There is a prize for the alivest-looking picture, and I want to get it." As he said this he threw open his studio door and there, seated in a chair, comfortably leaning back and smoking his pipe, was— who do you think? Why, old Mr Lizard himself, as large as life. Snugglepot rushed in and was just about to embrace him, when the artist caught him by the neck.

"What!" he cried, "you would spoil my picture. You rat! You bat! You native cat!" and he shook Snugglepot till his eyes jumped.

"Oh, oh!" cried poor Snugglepot, "I thought it was alive; it is my lost friend."

Then out from behind a long green curtain stepped old Mr Lizard. Snugglepot was overjoyed. There was great merriment at the artist's home that night. Dr Hokus Stickus came round to dinner, and everyone declared the picture to be livelike.

Now it happened that another artist in Big Bad had decided

to get the prize for the alivest picture, and most strange to say he had chosen for his model a Banksia man.

There was great excitement on the opening day. All the artists and other queer people went to see the pictures. When Snugglepot saw the portrait of the Banksia man it looked so real that he felt quite nervous. The great eye seemed to blink at him; he stood rooted with horror. Then suddenly the picture burst open, and out from the frame sprang the Banksia man, almost on top of him.

With a terrible yell the Banksia man seized Snugglepot by the legs and, scattering the people right and left, he ran from the gallery. The artist rushed out after him shouting "Murder! Help! Stop him!"

But the Banksia man's long legs covered the ground so quickly, and he turned so many different ways, that no one could catch him, and soon the shouts died away in the distance.

All this time poor Snugglepot's head was going round and round, and he nearly fainted with the pain of being carried upside down. It's very cruel to carry any live thing upside down, remember that!

In the Cave

Suddenly the Banksia man darted into a doorway and down a long passage, climbed a lot of steps, groped through a long, long dark tunnel, and came out into a cave at the end. In the cave were a number of Banksia men smoking, arguing, and playing bones. When they saw Snugglepot they all gathered round.

"Got 'im at last!" said the Banksia man, panting.

"Is he alive?" grunted one, poking Snugglepot with his horrible bony finger.

"Is 'e what?" sneered the Banksia man, tossing Snugglepot into a corner. "What'll we do with 'im, that's the question?"

"The little slimy sinner!" growled one.

"String and ring him!" said another.

"Rack and crack him!" snarled another.

"Bust and rust him!" croaked a monster with three eyes.

"Stick 'im on a bull-ant's nest; they'll kill 'im and the crows'll come and pick his bones," squeaked the smallest and ugliest of them all.

"Oh! Ah! Throw him to the bull-dogs," shouted all the Banksia men, jumping about in wicked glee.

"Give him a dose first," muttered one of them. So they opened poor Snugglepot's mouth and poured some horrible juice into it; and that was the last thing Snugglepot remembered.

*   *   *   *   *   *

Now old Mr Lizard, being a very sporting fellow, had sneaked off to the races instead of going to the picture-gallery with Snugglepot and the artist. When he came home, his cap on one side and swinging his cane jauntily, he was amazed to find Mrs Artist in tears, and Mr Artist saying the most dreadful words.

No sooner had the terrible news gone into his ears than he dashed out of the door. Old Mr Lizard was a sensible person, so he argued with himself as to which way the Banksia man would most likely have gone when he ran from the picture-gallery, and sure enough he guessed well, for as he passed a doorway he espied just inside upon the ground a little green cap. It was Snugglepot's; he knew it by the plans sticking inside.

In less time than it takes to tell, old Mr Lizard was standing outside the Banksia men's cave, breathing hard and listening.

"Well, come on," he heard one say, "if we're going to cop that slimy lizard we must be going."

Mr Lizard flattened himself against the wall; in his hands he held a heavy stick with a knobby end.

The first Banksia man came out into the dark passage. Whack went Mr Lizard's stick; and down went the Banksia man. "One!" muttered Mr Lizard under his breath, kicking the Banksia man to one side.

Out came another Banksia man. Whack went Mr Lizard's stick; down went the Banksia man. "Two!" whispered Mr Lizard.

Out came another Banksia man. Thud went Mr Lizard's stick; down went the Banksia man.

Out came another Banksia man. Whup went Mr Lizard's stick, and down went the Banksia man.

Out came two Banksia men together. Whack, whack, went Mr Lizard's stick. "Six," murmured Mr Lizard, swinging his stick.

No more Banksia men came; not a sound in the cave. Mr Lizard peeped in. Not a soul there. Yes, just one, poor little Snugglepot, lying still and white, his hands and feet tied and his eyes closed.

Alas! Poor Snugglepot

Mr Lizard stooped down—he started back. "Deadibones," he groaned. "Alas! Alas! Why did I go to the races?"

Then Mr Lizard flew into a passion of rage. Weeping and saying dreadful words, he pulled all the Banksia men into a heap in the middle of the cave and set fire to them.

Then, lifting Snugglepot tenderly in his arms, he fled from the place, moaning and weeping as he went.

And that really was the end of those wicked Banksia men.

With the Fish Folk

ALL this time Cuddlepie had been living happily with the Fish Folk, enjoying the wonderful sights and almost wishing he were a Fish Folk himself.

Ragged Blossom was so glad to have him. Ann Chovy and John Dory were so kind to him. Obelia was so wonderful; she was taller than Ann and wiser than ever.

One day while she was holding a council—for she was Queen of the Fish Folk now—there was a great commotion in the palace, and a prisoner was brought before her.

Throwing himself down, the Banksia man pleaded for mercy.

"What has he done?" asked Obelia. But without waiting for an answer she rose from her throne and hurried to her thinking-room. She had scarcely counted a lapful of pearls when she sprang up—and spilling the pearls as she ran, rushed into the council chamber.

"The villain!" she cried. "Throw him to the sharks. He and his black shadows have taken our Ragged Blossom; they have cast her into the bottomless sea, where the days are as nights—I have seen it. Throw him to the sharks! Away with him!"

At these words the councillors turned pale, for in Fish-folkdom no thought is so dreadful as the fear of the bottomless sea.

"There is just once chance," said Obelia. "Send Cuddlepie to the Fish Sauce shop."

"Alone?" gasped John Dory.

"Yes, alone," commanded Obelia.

A shudder ran through the council room.

"Give him his words and let him go," said Obelia. . . .

At the Races

(see page 207)

"What Has He Done?" asked Obelia

Trembling, but Brave, Cuddlepie Entered

Cuddlepie Is Brave

A little while later, Cuddlepie, trembling but brave, pushed his way through the great swing doors of the mysterious Fish Sauce shop.

As he went in, the shaggy head of a Banksia man peered out of a window. At the same moment a little black-and-white fish swam into a niche just over the doorway—it was Frilly.

"Say the words!" called a loud voice as Cuddlepie entered.

Cuddlepie started back. On each side and in front of him were the open mouths of hungry-looking fish; rows of sharp teeth glistened all round him.

"Say the words!" repeated the voice.

Cuddlepie was stiff with fear. He couldn't remember one word, yet he had said them over and over all the way.

"Too late! Eat him!" shouted the voice fiercely.

But just as the open mouths came at him, Cuddlepie made a great effort and began, "She—stood—at—the door—of the—fish—sauce—shop—welcoming—him—in."

At the first word the hungry fish turned; at the last word they vanished.

"Pass on!" called the voice.

Cuddlepie, still trembling but still brave, went through a huge archway of sharks' teeth and found himself in a beautiful white hall made of coral. All round the sides ran a little balcony, and in the middle of the floor was a deep black hole.

As Cuddlepie stood there wondering what the voice would say next, a strange and wonderful fish swam round the hall and stopped before him, on his head brilliant flashing lights of phosphorus, and harnessed with a bright red saddle from which hung a little sharp spear.

Right into the Monster's Throat

"Mount the messenger, take the spear, and be prepared to descend!" called the mysterious voice. Cuddlepie climbed into the saddle.

"Hold tightly to the messenger and say the words!" commanded the voice. Cuddlepie repeated the words.

At the sound of the last word the messenger dived into the black hole. Clinging to the harness with one hand and clutching his spear in the other—a terrible noise in his ears and a dreadful fear in his heart—Cuddlepie descended down, down, down into the bottomless sea. All was black dark. Cuddlepie shut his eyes; he could not bear to look at it.

Presently he opened them. All round him were flashing lights, and coming straight at him was a huge sea monster with fiery lights along his body and round his head, and the most terrible eyes and longest teeth Cuddlepie had ever seen.

Just as the great thing came rushing upon him, Cuddlepie lifted his spear and drove it right into the monster's throat. With a terrible gurgle it sank away into the dark. But before him was another great sea monster. Cuddlepie uttered a cry, for there, standing in its open mouth, all lit by the phosphorescence, stood little Ragged Blossom holding out her arms to him.

In a flash Cuddlepie had snatched her out, and the messenger turned his flashing headlights upwards. They rose and rose till suddenly they came right into the wonderful hall again. As they came to the edge of the balcony the great voice called, "Say the words!"

Now Cuddlepie was so excited at having found Ragged Blossom that he stammered out, "She—stood—at—the—door—of—the—fish—orse—shop—wel—cun—um—in—im."

Immediately there was a terrific explosion, then a black darkness.

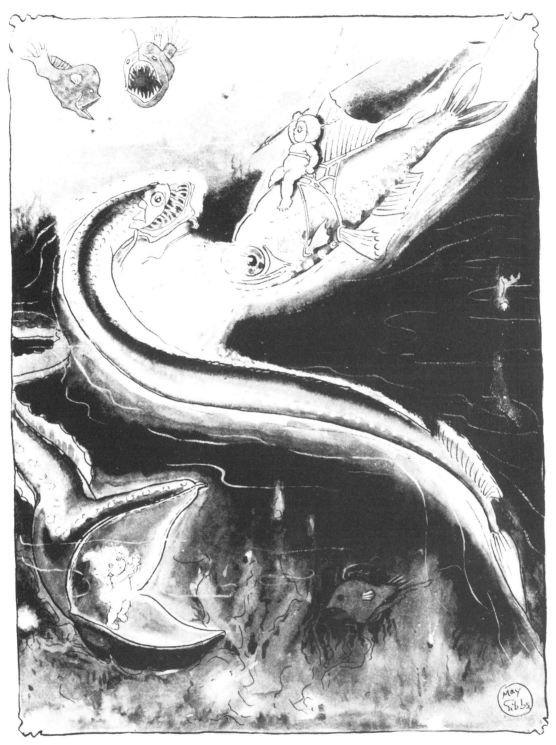

The Bottomless Sea

Frilly and Steady

THE sea was calm, and only a few rippling wavelets licked the small brown rock on which Ragged Blossom lay drying in the sun. Inquisitive sea-birds circled about her, while under the water little Frilly swam round and round the rock in an agony of mind.

He had patiently waited outside the Fish Sauce shop for Cuddlepie. Then came the terrible noise, and Frilly found himself thrown up to the surface of the sea. When he recovered from his fright he swam about looking for Cuddlepie and, spying along the top, he saw the sea-birds clustering about the rock.

"It must be Cuddlepie," he thought. When he found little Ragged Blossom lying there so still, he tried to leap onto the rock, calling "She will dry, she will dry."

A little Stormy Petrel hovering above him heard and understood. With a wail of sympathy he fluttered to her, caught her dress in his bill and pulled her into the sea.

With a shout of joy, Frilly caught her, and, calling to his little

Frilly Swam Round and Round

friend Steady, who was just swimming past, together they carried her home. Great was the rejoicing when they arrived with their burden. Ragged Blossom threw herself into Ann's arms, crying "Where is Cuddlepie?"

"Here I am," said Cuddlepie, kissing her.

"What was the terrible noise?" she asked.

"It was a seaquake," answered Obelia. "The Fish Sauce shop was blown apart, and all the Banksia men and the Giant Octopus have been thrown to the sharks."

"Who did that?" asked Ragged Blossom, shuddering.

"I did," said Obelia.

"How did Cuddlepie escape?" asked Ragged Blossom.

"It was the messenger," answered Obelia. "He is my own wonderful fish. You see, I laid a trap to catch the wicked Octopus."

"Why did I get blown up?" asked Ragged Blossom.

"It was an accident, dear little Gellyfish," said Obelia, smiling. "They will happen."

Alas! strange to tell, not many days later, when Cuddlepie and Ragged Blossom were walking in Ann's lovely garden, another accident happened. A great fish came rushing over the wall, his dark nose shining and his eyes glistening. Swift and straight he darted at the children, and before they could even cry out he had opened his huge jaws and swallowed them up. Then with a swish of his tail he turned and rushed away—away—away.

Inside the Fish

IT seemed a long, long time to Ragged Blossom and Cuddlepie; but it couldn't have been more than a few moments, because, almost immediately after the greedy fish swallowed them, he spied the bait on the end of Billy's line and snapped it up.

"Got him!" shouted Billy.

"Haul him in," said his father.

"A beauty!" chuckled Billy, as he swung the fish into the boat.

"He'll do nicely for lunch," said Billy's father. "I'll prepare him while you row in." Suddenly he sprang up. "Great Scott!" he exclaimed.

"What?" cried Billy, craning forward. "Oh, Father!" he gasped in amazement. "What can it be? Oh, Father! How wonderful!"

For there, in the middle of the opened fish, sat two tiny little creatures. It was Ragged Blossom and Cuddlepie. While Billy and his father stared with eyes and mouth wide open in utter astonishment, the little things jumped out and ran along the side of the boat.

Cuddlepie Glared at the Huge Face

Thoughtless Humans

"Catch 'em! Quick, Father! Catch 'em!" shouted Billy.

"Fill the specimen bottle and we'll put them in," said his father; and without waiting for lunch Billy and his father hurried home to show everyone their wonderful find.

Ragged Blossom and Cuddlepie clung together in the bottle as the great humans stared at them. Every now and then the big people shook the bottle to make them move, and their poor little heads were quite sore with being bumped against the sides.

"Just because we are little they think we can't feel," said Cuddlepie, glaring fiercely at the huge face of Billy, who simply did not know any better. At last, night came and the humans all went to bed.

"I hate humans!" said poor Cuddlepie, pushing at the heavy lid. "Come and help me, Ragged Blossom, it's moving."

After much struggling and straining they managed to lift the lid and clamber out. Then they slid down the tablecloth, ran along the floor, climbed up the window curtain, and in a moment were out on the sill of the open window.

The moon was shining. Sh! Sh! . . . Sh! Sh! . . . It was the voice of a possum walking along the bough of a gum-tree growing close beside the house.

"Mr Possum!" called Cuddlepie, trembling lest the humans should hear him.

What Happened at Mr Possum's House

"Hullo!" called back Mr Possum, lowering himself by his tail to see who it was.

"Take us into the tree," cried Ragged Blossom. "We're so frightened—the humans will catch us. Oh, quick!"

Reaching out his hands, Mr Possum swung them both up into the tree and took them safely to his little house in the Bush near by. By this time Ragged Blossom was so worn out and miserable that she fell upon Mrs Possum's motherly breast and wept.

"If—if—only dear Mr Lizard would come and take us home," she sobbed. "If only he were here!"

Now the strangest of strange things happened. The door opened and in walked old Mr Lizard, and who do you think was with him? Why, Snugglepot. When Mr and Mrs Possum saw all their visitors throwing their arms about each other's necks and talking and laughing and kissing and dancing about, they held up their hands in surprise.

"Get something to eat and drink, my dear," said Mr Possum, lighting his pipe.

It was nearly birdrise when Snugglepot, Cuddlepie and Ragged Blossom mounted Mr Lizard's back and said good-bye to kind Mr and Mrs Possum. After a long and happy journey the travellers arrived at Gumnut Town, and great was the rejoicing and great the amazement when the Nuts and Blossoms heard of the wonderful adventures.

"What became of all the Nuts who went with you?" they asked Cuddlepie. Alas! that is the sad part of the story; nobody ever knew.

Snugglepot built a new, big house, and took Cuddlepie and Ragged Blossom to live with him. Mr Lizard went off scouring the countryside for little Winky Jerboa. He found him lost and nearly starving. He brought him to Snugglepot, who rejoiced to see him and asked him to be his head gardener and live with him for always. Little Jerboa stuffed his tail into his mouth to hide his tears—he was so happy.

But Ragged Blossom missed her baby Obelia.

"She's not a baby; she's grown up," said Cuddlepie.

"But I'd like a baby," said Ragged Blossom.

"Well, sting and wing me!" cried Snugglepot. "You shall have one. Put on your hat and we'll go to the Baby shop."

It is the habit with the Gumnuts to gather up any little homeless Bush babies and take them to the Baby shop, so that anyone who wants to buy an extra baby or two may go to the shop and buy them.

Ragged Blossom was delighted, but when she got there she found it impossible to choose. "I love them all," she sighed.

"Then have the lot!" cried Snugglepot. "I've plenty of money," he added, slapping his cap. "When you and Cuddlepie were under the sea, Mr Lizard and I found the Banksia men's treasure."

"We'll buy the nurse too," suggested Cuddlepie.

"Good root!" said Snugglepot.

And so they did.

The Baby Shop

A Very Happy Family

And here is the end of the story of little Obelia. There wasn't really much about her in it, but what there was is very important, for if it hadn't been for the baby Obelia, Ragged Blossom wouldn't have stayed behind with the Fish Folk, and all these wonderful adventures would never have happened.

This is the Third Book of the Tales of Snugglepot and Cuddlepie.

THE END